THE MARKETING DIRECTOR'S ROLE

IN BUSINESS PLANNING AND

CORPORATE GOVERNANCE

THE MARKETING DIRECTOR'S ROLE

IN BUSINESS PLANNING AND

CORPORATE GOVERNANCE

Gerald Michaluk

John Wiley & Sons, Ltd

Other Wiley Editorial Offices

John Wiley & Sons Inc., 111 River Street, Hoboken, NJ 07030, USA

Jossey-Bass, 989 Market Street, San Francisco, CA 94103-1741, USA

Wiley-VCH Verlag GmbH, Boschstr. 12, D-69469 Weinheim, Germany

John Wiley & Sons Australia Ltd, 42 McDougall Street, Milton, Queensland 4064, Australia

John Wiley & Sons (Asia) Pte Ltd, 2 Clementi Loop #02-01, Jin Xing Distripark, Singapore 129809

John Wiley & Sons Canada Ltd, 6045 Freemont Blvd, Mississauga, ONT, L5R 4J3, Canada

Wiley also publishes its books in a variety of electronic formats. Some content that appears in print may not be available in electronic books.

Anniversary Logo Design: Richard J. Pacifico

British Library Cataloguing in Publication Data

A catalogue record for this book is available from the British Library

ISBN 978-0-470-51580-8 (HB)

Typeset in 11.5/15pt Bembo by SNP Best-set Typesetter Ltd., Hong Kong
Printed and bound in Great Britain by TJ International Ltd, Padstow, Cornwall, UK
This book is printed on acid-free paper responsibly manufactured from sustainable forestry in which at least two trees are planted for each one used for paper production.

Dedicated to all those managers that have welcomed me through their door over the years and to whom I am grateful for having had the privilege to work.

CONTENTS

ACKNOWLEDGEMENTS

This book has been made possible by the experience I have acquired over the last 27 years. The first company I was involved in forming while still a student was "Castle Ambulance Services Ltd", Scotland's first private ambulance company which, during the short time I was finance director, actually made money, but more importantly introduced me to the raw side of boardroom politics, power struggles and directorial conflict.

Since those early days I have worked with many more boards and found examples of excellent leadership, family conflict, and downright incompetence. To all those that provided me the experience I am grateful.

I have been greatly aided in the writing of this book by the staff at Marketing Management Services International. In particular I would like to thank Rikke Iversholt and Fred Moody for not just covering for me while I was locked away writing this work but for their significant contribution to its content.

Many have contributed to the book and I would like to thank David Grahame OBE MA of Linc Scotland, Robert Pattello of Archangels, Professor Donaldson and Bill Andrew.

Most importantly I would like to thank you, the reader, without whom this book would just be a dust catcher. I hope it will help you and give you new ideas that you can grow and develop making them your own and that this will benefit you and the organisations you choose to work with.

I am always interested in any idea you may have that will make this book more useful, so please send any suggestions to Gerald@marketingms.com, and please enter "marketing director" in the subject line.

ACRONYMS USED
IN THE TEXT

AGM	Annual General Meeting
BRC	British Red Cross
BS	Balanced Scorecard
C4ISR	Command, Control, Communications, Computers, Intelligence Surveillance and Reconnaissance
CA	Critical Assumption
CEO	Chief Executive Officer
CIA	Competitive Intelligence Acquisition
CIO	Chief Information Officer
CMO	Chief Marketing Officer
CPR	Customer Problem Resolution
CRM	Customer Relationship Management
DIKI	Data, Information, Knowledge and Intelligence
EGM	Extraordinary General Meeting
ENT	Enterprise Neuron Trails
ERP	Enterprise Resource Planning

FRC	Financial Reporting Committee
GMAS	Global Marketing Advantage System
IPO	Initial Public Offering
IT	Information Technology
KPI	Key Performance Indicator
KRA	Key Result Area
MBBS	Management by Best Seller
MI	Marketing Intelligence
MMSI	Marketing Management Services International
NLP	Neuro Linguistic Programming
P/E	Price/earnings ratio
PA	Personal Assistant
PR	Public Relations
RoI	Return on Investment
SaaS	Software as a Service
SFA	Sales Force Automation
STORM	Strategic Tactical Operational Review Management
TPV	Third Party Vendors
USP	Unique Selling Proposition

CHAPTER 1

BOARD LEVEL IMPLICATIONS

If you contrive each day to outclass the fellow you were yesterday, reaching the top is just a matter of time.

Source: Unknown

Whether you are a new member of the board, the managing partner in a major firm, or a student, this book will help you to understand the role of marketing at the organisation's governing level.

Specifically we will consider the role of the marketing director, chief marketing officer or any other title that describes the person responsible for guiding the board in the area of marketing. This will include the interpretation of marketing research in relation to corporate strategy, and consideration of the director's responsibilities in the governance of the organisation as a whole.

The book will refer, in the main, to the board of directors or corporate officers "C-level" executive, but the basic role is synonymous with that of the managing partners, trustees of a charity or management team of a government agency. Thus, if you fall into any of the latter categories please read the term "director" in its widest context and with regard to your own organisation's governance.

THE ROLE OF THE BOARD OF DIRECTORS

In an Act of Parliament in 1844 directors were described as "the persons having the direction, conduct, management or supervision of a company's affairs".

A company is a "Person" in the eyes of the law and can perform many of the functions of a living person; for example, own property, enter into contracts, be taken to court. However, it is clearly not a real person and therefore is often described as an "Article" in as much as it can act only through its agents. Those agents make up the board of directors. Put another way, those who exercise effective control over the company's affairs are referred to as the board of directors. The number of directors required varies by the type of company, Plc or Ltd, and by the country in which the company is domiciled. A minimum number of directors is often required.

In a very small company the role of the marketing director may be shared with other roles such as finance director, managing director or chief cook and bottle washer, while in medium-sized and larger organisations it is normal to have either a part-time or full-time marketing director. The nomenclature for the post may vary, ranging from the "Sales and Marketing Director" to the "Chief Marketing Officer".

The role and power of the directors, as well as election and retirement rules, are to be found in the company's Articles of Association, while the Memorandum of Association defines and regulates the company and its dealings with the outside world. The internal constitution, and hence rules within which the board are empowered to act, is documented in the Articles of Association. It is imperative that, as a director, you know the content and scope of both of these documents and work within their limitations or have them altered to permit the required actions. Changing any of these documents will involve a resolution and approval by the members (shareholders), not just the board of directors.

The functions of the board are:

- Deciding policy
- Safeguarding the shareholders' investment
- Safeguarding the employees
- C4ISR (see below)
- Compliance with regulations.

Deciding policy

The company needs direction and the board of directors provide the strategic leadership of the company. They formulate the mission, vision and values of the organisation and prepare the strategic plans.

Safeguarding the shareholders

The board of directors are the servants of the shareholders, and they must not only ensure the shareholders' best interests by providing a return on their investment, but must also safeguard the firm's long-term survival.

Safeguarding the employees

The directors are held responsible for the safe working environment they provide for their employees and, as such, must ensure that employees are treated in a just, fair and unbiased manner throughout the organisation.

C4ISR

This is an acronym taken from the military and refers to Command, Control, Communications, Computers, Intelligence, Surveillance and Reconnaissance. In the corporate context this means ensuring the growth of the company by keeping its operations under constant review and making any necessary changes without delay when necessary. Constantly comparing results with expectations and reconciling them ensures the efficient and effective operation of the company.

Compliance with regulations

Increasingly new legislation and international agreements appear under a myriad of disguises: for example, Sarbanes Oxley, anti-money laundering, regulations means that company directors are increasingly being held personally liable for the actions of their organisation, and hence must have failsafe controls in place to ensure compliance with the increased bureaucracy involved in running any company regardless of size.

THE MARKETING DIRECTOR AS A LEADER

I must follow them; I am their leader – (ET Raymond)

Within the above roles there are three ingredients to which we must pay particular attention:

- Leadership
- Responsibility
- Accountability

To lead means to empower efficient and effective action to those who are accountable to you. It is important to understand that you are responsible, while those whom you have chosen to act on your behalf are accountable to you.

If a plan fails, then you must take responsibility, because you entrusted the execution of that plan to others who failed in its achievement. If the plan is successful, it will have been through the action of others and hence the credit for success lies with them, and not with you. To be a leader, therefore, is not a glorious position. If you are successful, others must be given the credit, and when they fail you must take the blame.

Others may be held accountable for their action, but failure is firmly the responsibility of the leadership.

TYPES OF DIRECTOR

The board may be made up of a number of distinct types of director.

- Excutive directors
- Non-executive directors
- Alternative directors

The role of the executive directors

The executive directors work for the company in a full time capacity and are rewarded normally in the form of salary, fees and/or bonus scheme. The contracting of directors is a complex area and there are several law firms that can advise in this area. Rather like a footballer, it can be beneficial to have an agent handle this aspect on your behalf – especially if your skills are in short supply.

The role of the non-executive directors

These are normally part-time members, from outside the company, who attend board meetings, provide specialist input and serve on committees where their outsider view can balance the full-time directors' day-to-day internal management view.

The role of alternative directors

It is normal for the Articles of Association to allow directors to have someone else acting on their behalf when they cannot attend a board meeting in person. There is a procedure set down in the Memorandum/Articles of Association and this should be consulted to define how alternative directors are appointed and the authority they can exercise. (See Appendix 1 for a sample of Memorandum and Articles.)

Special considerations

Whether we are talking about a limited company (Ltd), a public limited company (Plc), or their equivalents in other countries, the basic role of a director is the same, with the only differences being reporting requirements, size of pay check and impact of getting it right or wrong.

The trustees of a charity

Many charities have a constitution similar to a company's Memorandum of Association and Articles of Association, and the trustees perform the role of the board of directors, ensuring that the charity focuses on achieving its purpose.

Partnerships

There are limited and non-limited partnerships. Where a partnership exists there is normally a partnership agreement, which outlines how the partnership functions. Should there be no formal partnership agreement there is a statutory default agreement that will form the basis in law of the relationship. Limited partnerships are very similar in governance to a limited liability company and are managed by the senior partners or a committee sometimes elected by the partners.

Family-run businesses

Family-run businesses are a complete book in themselves. There is a lot more to be considered when you are involved in one as an outsider or as a family member. The old terms "Governing Director", "Life Director" or "Permanent Director" were often used to describe the special powers that founders reserved for themselves – for example, not requiring to retire by rotation, or having no age limit for retirement. Thus, the company may be a dictatorship with other directors playing second fiddle to the master.

There are nevertheless some extremely successful family-run companies that have survived many generations and continue to prosper. Regrettably in the UK they are in the minority, with many failing after the initial founding generation retires.

In order to run a family business you must be strong enough to separate the three core elements found in the business: management, ownership and family.

Many family businesses have survived to the detriment of the family members who work in them, while others have a job only because they are in a family business. A real employer would have fired such people in the first month, but uncle Fred can not do that because of the family connection. On the other hand, I have seen very talented individuals being forced into working in the family business and earning less than a quarter of their worth.

A split personality

The governance of family businesses needs special attention on the three antagonistic considerations of management, ownership and family. These three elements have to be balanced if a successful organisation is to survive and flourish from one generation to the next. Rather like the alchemist, turning base metal into gold, these three base elements can, in the right hands, be turned into generational wealth but, in the wrong hands, they can turn gold into lead overnight.

The balance of these goals will set the organisation's objectives but the business must be prepared for this balance to shift over time. It is imperative to optimise all three and avoid dominance of any one, which is not an easy task where emotions, tradition, loyalty and feeling of birthright are involved.

In order to achieve a successful solution the three roles must be separated from each other and there are a number of consultancies, such as Marketing Management Services International Ltd, who can take a family business through this painful process.

Management

The secret of management is to separate family and ownership from the decisions that need to be made to optimise the organisation's function. Once you have determined the skills that are needed, they should be hired via an objective selection process, bringing outsiders in if necessary to ensure that the right person gets the job. Family members may be encouraged to gain the skills required for the job but they should be evaluated on the basis of suitability and past performance, and nothing else. This is very easy to say but very difficult in the real world to implement. When a family business is formed it should be grooming the next generation very early, thereby ensuring that they are encouraged in the right direction, that their natural talents are maximised and that the business education and training needed is provided to tomorrow's managers. (Goldman Sachs, for example, was very successful as a family business.)

Ownership

After several generations there will be distant cousins that have shares in the firm and have, perhaps, paid little attention to the business apart from attending the AGM and asking yet again why there have been no dividend payments. Shareholders should be treated respectfully and the director's duty is to ensure that they receive a fair return for their investment. There are generally industry ratio analysis providers who report sector norms, and these ratios should be used to determine if the shareholders are getting an honest return for their investment in the company. There are huge advantages to having loyal shareholders, and although family members make up one of the strongest groups of loyal shareholders, it does not mean that they should be taken for granted or exploited.

Family

In reality, the business is there to support the family and, therefore, there are going to be family considerations and a high degree of nepotism. But the business should not divide the family, and the family should not sacrifice too much for the business. The relationship between family and business should be realistic. If cousin Bill is not going to be happy working in the business, it is not in the family's interest to force him into a role for which he is not suitable, or make him feel guilty if he pursues some other occupation. However, the family members should grow wealthier through the business and be encouraged to participate if they show an interest.

There is not enough time to discuss all the intricacies of governing a family business, but the simple division of the core elements and their individual maximisation is a very powerful starting point. The remainder of the book is as applicable to family-run companies as it is to any other type of organisation.

THE MANAGING DIRECTOR

While you may, by now, be feeling that the role the marketing director is expected to perform is tough to master, spare a thought for the managing director or chairman. The mind map below outlines that individual's role in chairing meetings alone.

For the formal procedure of a meeting of the board or governing body, see Appendix 2. Although in reality meetings are usually less formal than that described in the appendix, that is not always the case.

If the managing director and chairman do their jobs well, you can concentrate on your marketing role; however, that role will be made considerably more difficult if other members of the board do not perform their roles as you are all mutually dependent on each other.

- Effective boards do not carry passengers, while ineffective boards are so full of passengers it is difficult to do anything other than talk.
- Effective boards get things done through others; ineffective boards talk and hope it will work out all right.
- Effective boards are ahead of the business; ineffective boards never catch up with it and, if they do, it's because the company went into liquidation.

Thus, the secret of being a star is to be on a board full of stars. Very few stars can survive in an ineffective board as they are too big a threat to the status quo. I am sorry to say that I have found this to be particularly true in government-sponsored projects

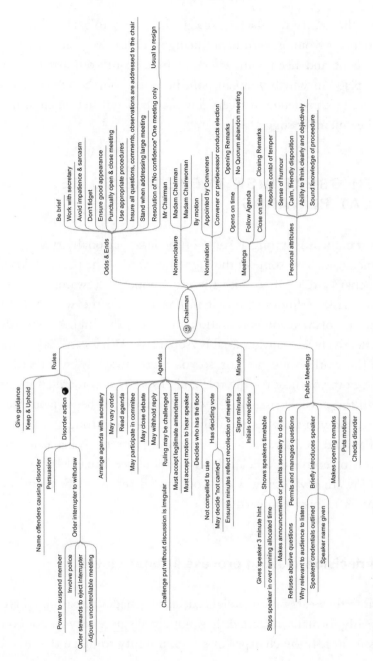

Figure 1.1 Mind map of the role of the chairman of the board

where the ability to talk far exceeds the ability to act or manage. Therefore, avoid government quangos unless you are nearing retirement and need somewhere to hide from your partner, or some place in which you can pontificate to your heart's content, safe in the knowledge that very few members will act on anything another member suggests.

WITH GREAT RISK THERE HAS TO BE GREAT REWARDS

This statement is wrong as some of the least personally risky governance roles have some of the highest rewards. The person taking on a charity role, often with the least monetary rewards, has the highest risk of finding himself in court, while the well-insured executive of a major corporation can have the highest rewards for effectively very little actual personal risk. What can I say other than the world is just not fair, so you must always assess the situation before you take on any role and ensure that you are aware of the all the possible risks. Just because you are not being paid does not release you from responsibility if things go wrong.

Pay and perks raise other interesting points. What can you expect to receive in a board level position (see Table 1.1)?

Now that we know what you should receive, let's turn our attention to how you earn it.

The decision-making process at board level

Because they carry more weight, decisions made at board level are normally formally recorded. It is not always necessary to vote on an issue as it is the chairperson's responsibility to judge the mood of the meeting. However, on some issues votes are cast either anonymously or by a simple show of hands.

Table 1.1 Pay for executive marketing directors 2006

	Lower quartile (£)	Median (£)	Upper decile (£)	Sample size
Basic salary	54,420	73,750	116,982	116
Remuneration	57,608	78,665	131,060	116
Bonus	6,000	12,000	42,000	49
Age	38	43	55	92

Company car

Percentage of directors with company car	24%
Percentage with free private mileage	19%
Maximum list price of car allowed	£30,000

Pensions and insurance

Life Assurance	4 times salary
Percentage with health insurance	63%
Percentage with permanent health insurance	45%
Employees pension rate	3%
Company pension rate	5%

Source: The Marketing Managers Yearbook 2007

What the board is being asked to approve should have been considered in some depth and will have a sponsor at board level, the person bringing it to their attention. Other "sign-offs" are compliance related, e.g. approving the accounts before presentation at the Annual General Meeting of the company.

It is neither possible, nor necessary, for the board of directors to review all the detail but by approving the resolution, they are taking responsibility for it.

There is a lot of confusion about accountability and responsibility and, at the risk of repeating myself, they are quite easily separated. The board of directors are responsible individually and collectively for those reporting to them. Those that report to you are accountable to you for their actions, and this passes on through the chain of command. As you are responsible for your choice of leaders, and have entrusted them with the task, then if something goes wrong through their mistakes or their sheer incompetence, you are responsible as you appointed them.

Too many board members avoid responsibility and employ scapegoat tactics, blaming those reporting to them. Such members are weak leaders, although, I might add, they are not always unsuccessful.

The true leader takes responsibility when things go wrong and acknowledges and credits others for success. This is completely contrary to what we see in politics, where credit is taken for any successes and the previous governments are blamed for any failures.

COMPANY MINUTES AND RESOLUTIONS

Meetings of the board, other than committees, take three forms: board meetings, the Annual General Meeting (AGM) and the Extraordinary General Meeting (EGM).

A board meeting is the regular meeting of the board. This ranges from monthly to quarterly, depending on the size of the company and the issues the company is facing. You exercise your power as a director through voting at board meetings and signing resolutions.

Board meeting AGMs and EGMs all require reasonable notice. The period is defined in company law and/or in the Articles of Association. One person, one vote, is customary in board meetings, and there must be a quorum (minimum number of directors present). Minutes must be taken and held in the Company Register. In the case of the AGM and the EGM to which shareholders are invited, votes are based on voting shares. A person who owns 20,000 shares has 20,000 votes while you, as a director – who may not be required to own shares – may effectively have no votes. Some resolutions, e.g. changing the Articles of Association, can only be passed if this is agreed by a certain percentage of all those eligible to vote.

What all these meetings have in common is the keeping of minutes and recording of resolutions passed. As these are legal documents, some of them require to be filed in the Company Register and others with the Registrar of Companies.

SUMMARY

- The marketing director has the same roles and responsibilities as any other director and has to be familiar with that role and its limitations and responsibilities.
- Family-run businesses need special consideration.
- To be successful, choose to join a board made up of stars, but as you win or lose as a team, you should therefore play as a team.

The size of the company and the specific point in a firm's growth curve will determine the exact nature and role required of the marketing director. This will be discussed in the next chapter.

CHAPTER 2

WHO DO WE SERVE AS DIRECTORS?

Marketing is the management process responsible for identifying, anticipating and satisfying customer requirements profitably.

The Chartered Institute of Marketing

In your new role as marketing director, you will need to establish who are your new customers groups, because you now have an expanded audience consisting of not just end-customers for your product or services, but a range of others who have often as much impact on the organisation as your intrinsic customers.

To help to understand who these new audiences are, it is helpful to draw up a publics map or stakeholders' map. Each of the stakeholders will have some kind of exchange-based relationship with your organisation and therefore we will need to understand our image from their perspective. Obviously some stakeholders are far more important than others, but they all impact on the company and hence marketing will have to consider how to identify, anticipate and satisfy their needs profitably from the company's perspective.

SURVEYING THE ORGANISATION

It would be nice to think that there is only one perspective on everything but, of course, in the real world, as in the world of *Alice in Wonderland*, there are many perspectives.

Looking at the publics or stakeholders of any organisation, we can see that each has a specific and often self-interested view of the role of the marketing director or chief marketing officer (CMO). This would be complicated enough, but their expectation changes with the stage of the organisation's growth, market conditions and other macro- or micro-economic considerations. For example, bear or bull stock markets can change what investors want from the organisation.

PUBLICS MAPS

One of the fundamental mistakes of many new marketing directors is that they do not consider the customer's perspective despite being customer focused in their previous marketing role. The old question "Who is the customer?" needs to be asked, but from the context of the whole organisation and its exchange relationships. In order to answer this question you must first map the marketing organisation's interactions internally and externally. We soon find a multitude of connections.

Figure 2.2 shows a very simplified map for the British Red Cross's exchange processes, which I shall use to show the nature of the relationships.

The British Red Cross (BRC) helps the needy by providing, in this example, volunteers. There is therefore a relationship

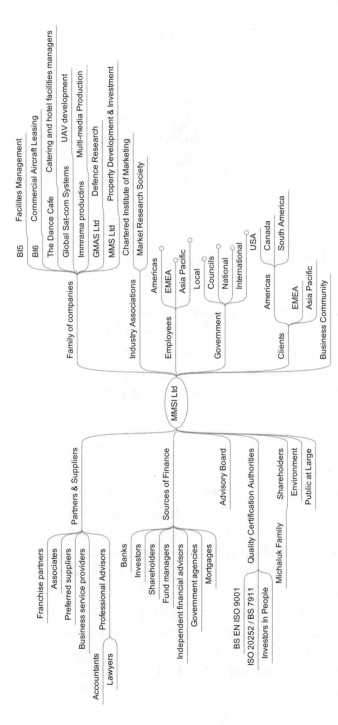

Figure 2.1 Publics map/stakeholders map

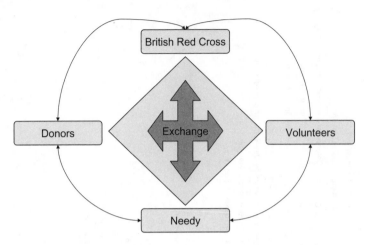

Figure 2.2   Simplified publics map

between the BRC and the volunteer. Similarly, there is a relationship between the volunteer and the needy. In addition, there is
also a need for the BRC to get the funds required to help the
needy and because, in this case, the funds come from the public
(you and me) we too have a relationship with the needy. All of
these relationships, or interactions, have an exchange process
attached to them. For example, the volunteers give up their time,
learn new skills and provide a service for the BRC. What does the
BRC provide them with in exchange? If you have ever been for-
tunate enough to work with these exceptional people, you will
know that they have a range and mixture of motives for working
for a charity. Motives can range from guilt – perhaps not having
been able to help at the scene of an accident – through enhanced
self-image to truly altruistic motives. The BRC caters for a wide
range of needs. Similarly, there is an interaction between the volunteer and those being helped, and the public and the BRC. Each
one has a complex set of interchanges which, if mutually beneficial,
will continue. However, when a volunteer is asked to give too
much, then the relationship breaks down. Each year some of the

elderly in our society die from hypothermia rather than ask for help. Help at the cost of loss of pride may be too high a price for them to pay. Therefore, in order for an agency such as the BRC to help, it must first ensure that it considers each of these interchanges.

Publics maps draw out these relationships and allow the nature of the exchange and the balance to be considered. For example, the customer is the person that relatively gains least and parts with the most, as is the case of any trade. Put simply, you have a customer if you profit from the relationship. Thus the BRC has three customer groups: the public, the volunteers, and the needy. The BRC profits from the work of the volunteers, it achieves its mission by helping the needy and it gains its funds from the public. In all three relationships the BRC profits. Therefore it is in the BRC's interest to treat each of these groups as customers, to understand and monitor the relationships and to strategically plan for the long term so that it can maximise its "profit" from the public or stakeholders. Here, again, perspective plays a key role as each party has a different objective. So ideally for the partnership to continue, each party must believe it is gaining the maximum benefit from the relationship. Therefore, to sustain an initial relationship, you require several elements:

- A continued need
- A satisfactory customer experience
- Awareness
- Opportunity
- Resources
- High perceived value
- Trust
- Tendency to loyalty
- Mutual profit/benefit
- Authority

- Authorisation within the corporate policy
- Excitement.

Many customers are lost and opportunities missed because a firm has been unaware that interactions between these elements are essential for a continued relationship to establish and grow. When the value of the interactions is realised, personal relationships become an important factor.

The second advantage of a publics map is that you can determine where the relationship is not profitable from your company's perspective. These are areas where you can make savings.

Ideally, you will want relationships to be mutually profitable. By this it is meant that both sides of the exchange should believe that they are achieving profits. This has been done very effectively by the BRC, because profits are multi-perspective items. Labour may be considered by a volunteer to be less valuable than the sense of achievement that is gained from helping others; while for the BRC, giving a sense of achievement to its volunteers may be relatively easily achieved, compared to the cost of employing, managing and motivating staff to undertake the work carried out by the volunteers. With both parties treating each other as the customer, a mutually beneficial partnership is born.

A third benefit is what you don't see when you draw up your publics map. On a creative thinking course being conducted by one of my clients, one of my exercises was to draw a plant. Art was not my strong point at school and you can imagine the outcome – I think a 5-year-old could have done better! The class was then instructed to stop trying to draw the plant, but instead draw the spaces around the plant. What a difference. I produced a much more recognisable drawing of the plant, which came as a great surprise. Often the surrounding spaces are more important than the object that fills your view, and what is missing from the publics map is just as revealing. What should I see? What relationships are we missing out on?

Publics mapping is a vital ingredient in gaining a true understanding of the relationships between your marketing function and its stakeholders and should be drawn out early in the planning process.

COMPANY STAKEHOLDERS

In a limited company the key stakeholders are (1) the end customers for products and services, (2) shareholders, (3) financiers and bankers, and (4) staff. Let's look at each and explore the relationship a little further.

The end customers

This is the bread and butter of marketing, and as you will have had considerable experience in this area I do not propose to dwell on it here.

Shareholders

As you will recall, the board of directors are entrusted by the shareholders to run the company. Therefore, the shareholders are collectively your ultimate boss. Just as with your line manager, the better you manage the shareholders the easier your life will be, so you should develop a marketing strategy aimed at recruiting the "right" kind of investor.

Short-term and quarterly horizons

The wrong kinds of shareholder will have a very negative impact on the business. For example, how can you prepare long-term plans if you can't invest in the future because of shareholders' pressure for short-term gains. Similarly, you will always be vulnerable to an unwelcome takeover unless you have the right mix of shareholders that can be mobilised to thwart any such attempt.

As much as 50% of the managing director's/chief executive officer's time can be spent dealing with markets and providing analysts with information that is often not in the best interest of the company to reveal. There are many examples of companies being persuaded to reveal too much of their plans to the market analysts and, as you probably know, the best source of competitor intelligence can be found in the shareholders' section of corporate websites. Recently I found a competitor's complete strategic presentation, including detailed market research justifications of their strategic direction. This saved us several thousand pounds in research costs and confirmed that our own strategy was sound. Marketing to investors is a critical role and, in my view, should involve the best marketing mind in the organisation – that is, YOU.

Shareholder loyalty

Well over a decade ago writers, such as Frederick Reichheld in his book *The Loyalty Effect*, were describing the fact that some shareholders and institutional investors were more inherently loyal than others and that a wise firm should seek out loyal shareholders just as they do loyal customers. His basic argument was simple: If you want to reduce share price volatility, then actively pursue investors with a high loyalty tendency. Examples of firms that have pursued this strategy are MBNA and A.G. Edwards, among others.

The complexity of life is reflected in the many differing motives behind the various investors, some of whom are more easily classified than others. An analysis of the market can provide lists of investors whose motives are aligned with your company, and it is interesting to note that several writers have claimed that these very loyal investors are also the ones that, over the long term, make the most money and have the most consistent results.

- *The business angels:* Traditionally the business angels get involved at the early stage of a company's development and seek an exit after two or three years. They can range from working investors, i.e. buying themselves a job for a few years, to hands-on investors, taking a chance on a new idea.
- *Venture capitalists:* These tend to be in the mid-market but can finance some very large investments. However, they are inclined to exit on flotation.
- *Institutional investors:* These are the fund managers that have millions to find a home for each month with various different objectives ranging from capital growth to income generation and everything in between.
- *Private investors and investment syndicates:* These people are looking for companies in which they can invest to bring them capital growth and or dividends. Included in this group are the day traders and the share builder scheme members – a real mixture of loyal and transient investors.
- *Employee investors:* Many companies find this a very attractive group as they tend to be loyal and have ownership, which has a positive impact on motivation at work. Many workers don't mind seeing the company's money wasted, but when they feel it is their own money they take a very different view.
- *Influencers such as analysts, the media and industry groups:* As I mentioned, as much as 50% of the managing director's time is spend dealing with these groups and a slip of the tongue can have adverse effects on the company. The best known, if somewhat dated, example being Mr Ratner, whose jewellery chain collapsed as a result of a throw-away line about the quality of his goods.

Is it possible to fool the analysts? Yes! ask any Enron Executive. Are they fair and impartial? Most certainly not, Do they have favourites? Yes. Can they be hostile? Yes. Can they make or break your company? Yes.

Investor relations is seriously important and the marketing director must ensure that investors receive the right messages. It is also an area in which specialist knowledge is required as there are regulations governing what can and cannot be said, when it can be said, and when it cannot be said. The fallout from Enron makes this area one in which it is best to seek current advice.

Financiers and bankers

Few companies can get by without recourse to external sources of finance, other than shareholder capital. This means that the relationship in which you may consider yourself the client is in fact one in which it pays you to manage. Building relationships is vital, and ensuring that you are informed of new offers ahead of the competition and the possibility of a beneficial rate of interest is very important. If the relationship grows unmanaged, you will find that a less than optimal situation quickly develops.

You have to be careful in this situation because the CFO (chief financial officer) or finance director has direct responsibility for this area. As the marketing director, you should ensure that his/her job is made easier by providing intelligence on rates enjoyed by competitors. You should also ensure that the institutions receive a consistent picture of the health of the company and not gain their knowledge from rumour or non-managed sources.

It is quite normal for competition in the banking sector to result in offers being available from time to time that you could happily have taken advantage of if you had only been aware of them. As they say, you are the first to know about price rises but the last to know that you could have been paying less. In my own property company we were paying 2.5% above base and it was only after checking on competitors that we discovered they were getting 2% above base. It took only one meeting to have that rectified, generating considerable savings in finance costs. Our finance director had not spotted the opportunity to squeeze the rates as she had no means of knowing the rate being given to our competitors and did not consider networking a particularly valuable use of her time. The information needs to be provided by the person responsible for competitor intelligence and it is that person's job to help to furnish other members of the board with information that will help them do their jobs better. The person who is relied upon to have the pulse of the market is the marketing director. YOU.

The moral of the story is that if we had had a better relationship we could have achieved the better rate without requesting it. We learned our lesson.

Staff

This, too, is an area in which the marketing director should be involved but there may be a personnel director who feels that this is their patch. While the policy on employment, etc., is most definitely their responsibility, the internal communications function should be under the control of marketing to ensure that one single corporate voice is established consistently internally and externally. Too many companies give very different messages to their staff, their shareholders and their customer, and wonder why people get confused. The angle of messages can be very different but the core strategy must be communicated consistently and the flow of market intelligence must be coordinated and disseminated. Too many people doing similar jobs makes no sense. On investigating why some companies fail I often hear that everyone knew what was happening except those who needed to know and could have acted to prevent the damage. Market intelligence should to be available where it is needed, and centrally analysed and disseminated.

Advisers

The benefits of external advisers and consultants cannot be under-estimated, nor can the dangers of their over-use be emphasised strongly enough. External advisers bring a new perspective to the company and allow it to gain knowledge and expertise that it does not have in house. However, like the Ancient Romans and their use of mercenaries, it can be dangerous if you put all your trust in them alone.

The secret is a good brief that provides the necessary background and a good working relationship. Use them to achieve the objectives and learn from the consultants, but never become dependent upon them.

GROWTH IN CONSUMERISM

It is not now enough to abide by the laws, but it is important that you are seen to do so and that your operations and conduct of business are above reproach. The growth in consumer power and a host of media campaigners can put considerable pressure on an organisation or even government. In the UK the Chancellor had to back down on proposed fuel surcharges when activists mobilised and blockaded fuel depots. At the time of writing he is proposing a similar move and has ensured there will not be a repetition of events.

THE BIG PICTURE

As you may have surmised, my view of marketing is that it is involved in all aspects of the organisation from investor relations, through public relations to individual product branding. As the embodiment of the marketing ethos on the board, you will now have to consider many more aspects of marketing than you have done at any previous time in your marketing career.

I am sure at some time in your marketing career you will have questioned why there is so much red tape about what you could or could not do. Much of that will have evolved as a result of trying to ensure a corporate image that is acceptable to all stakeholders, even if it means the sub-optimisation of some operational marketing activities.

Rather like sacrificing a pawn to achieve check-mate in a game of chess, it is winning the game that counts not the number of pieces you still have on the board. Therefore, one of the most difficult things you have to do is detach yourself from any individual aspect of the organisation's marketing. This is often difficult, as you probably have come from some operational marketing role of which, not surprisingly, you have a great understanding and hold in some high regard. It is time to revisit the textbook and refamiliarise yourself with all aspects of marketing, with particular emphasis on areas in which you have not had an operational involvement. You need to understand how all the sections function and how they can be used together.

Like a game of chess, you must always consider your options before a move and try to anticipate the likely reaction of your opponent. It is necessary to consider how any individual marketing activity will impact on the organisation as a whole. To satisfy shareholders' thirst for information you don't want to compromise your entire marketing strategy. Many firms have fallen into this trap where public relations or investor relations have given away too much information. As I have already stated, the first place I look for competitor information is investors relations, newsletter and press releases, and I am always surprised by the detail provided. There is a fine balance between keeping the investors informed and compromising future strategy.

To illustrate the point of difference in expectation even looking at similar groups, let's look at some investors. You can see areas of similarity and areas of contrast.

What do investors want from the marketing director?

We have talked at length about the importance of the investors, so what are their views on the role of the marketing director? Investors' views vary depending on the stage of the company's growth, but here are typical views.

David Grahame has a local investment networking company that marries entrepreneurs with Business Angels in Scotland. I have summarised his views as follows:

> New companies are quite often managed by inventors or engineers that have developed a new product and are looking for a market. The founder has had to deal with marketing as well as all the other tasks. There is a need to switch from being product led to market led and this is the primary role of a new marketing director. The marketing director must direct the next generation of product to a specific market.

We have Scottish-based firms that only sell to the USA because the buying process for the medical product in the UK is not favourable. Channel selection is vital, as is a strategic focus, it is not just a matter of getting sales. Although in the early stages of development the marketing director will most likely be expected to organise and be actively involved in sales, this must not be done exclusively as it is important that the directors sets the marketing vision for the firm.

In another company, a traditional boat builder had to learn how to make fibreglass boats owing to the fall in demand for wooden boats. The marketing director saw a firm that was a fibreglass expert not a boat builder, and the firm has grown enormously making fibreglass sheds.

The Business Angels investors are expected to bring both financial skills and marketing skills to the table and therefore they have a great deal of influence in the selection of the marketing directors. It should also be noted that it is quite normal in this size of company for the post of marketing director to be part time in the first instance.

Robert Pattullo of Archangels, one of the largest business angel investment syndicates in Scotland, takes the following view:

> Archangels, mainly, deal with early stage high-tech companies and have very specific views on the role of the marketing director. They must be able to sell to big corporations, and this is no easy task for a young company with no track record or even a stable balance sheet. They require to have: relevant industrial experience, a profile in the industry, and a thorough knowledge of the market. They are introduced before the marketing plan is finalised and the product is launched and play a vital role in defining the channels to market as well as contributing to the company's overall business and marketing plan.

Robert defines their role in the business and marketing planning exercise as "providing the key to the art of the possible" – separating what the company would like to do from what is possible in the market.

The role in the small high-tech company is definitely both sales and marketing and, if anything, it is sales first. Given the choice of recruiting a marketing manager or a sales manager wanting to enter marketing, the sales manager would get the appointment provided he had no illusions about leaving his sales role behind. The new director must know his way around large corporations and, together with the chairman, have credibility. He is most likely to be selling business-to-business and developing the channel to market. He will have no role in investor relations, this being dealt with by the CEO, but will be involved to the extent of ensuring that good news PR is delivered to the trade press and on the website.

I would estimate that there is a broad agreement on the role of marketing director, but a marketed difference on emphasis depending on the stage of investment. It is mainly about marketing, but it is also about sales, and regardless of the limited view of some individuals that selling is beneath them, the marketing director's role involves a high degree of sales skills from selling ideas to selling product. Sales is firmly part of the marketing role and those who separate the two are dreaming. The aim of marketing may be, as Drucker said, to "make selling superfluous", but until it does, the director must get used to having to make sales.

SUMMARY

- The role is based on understanding the various areas in which marketing benefits the organisation.
- The nature, size, maturity and market conditions influence the role, as does the growth cycle.
- Understanding the publics and the exchange relationships is key to being successful.
- Different people have very different views on what the role is, so define your own in the light of others' expectations.

CHAPTER 3

THE TOOLS AND AIDS AVAILABLE TO THE MARKETING DIRECTOR

The girl who can't dance says the band can't play.

Yiddish proverb

It is essential to have the right tools for the job. If you have ever tried to do DIY you will know that if you are using the wrong tools the task will take twice as long and never quite turn out the way it should. Therefore, to avoid unnecessary effort and poor results, we need to ensure access to the best marketing tools we can afford.

The tools enable marketing directors to bring their attention to the priority issues and free up their time. Time is the key ingredient of which there is never enough. Time is the ultimate resource. Given time we can do anything; however, we are given very little on this Earth – only three score years and ten – and in the corporate environment we have very much less time but a great deal to achieve. As a marketing director you will now need to manage your time better than at any other stage of your career.

TIME MANAGEMENT

Time management is critical. All the host of techniques from speed-reading to efficient diary/calendar management and personal filing need to be mastered. You can find all your time taken up by meetings, and do little else if you are not careful. One of the essential skills you must master is handling meetings and ensuring that they are both effective and efficient.

Jack Gratus, in his book *Give and Take*, provides a list of good reasons for having meetings:

- To bring people together
- To aid communications
- To inspire
- To energise
- To air grievances
- To pool resources
- To get you noticed.

He also points out some poor reason, and meetings for these reasons must be avoided as they are a waste of your valuable time:

- To avoid responsibility
- To display power
- Out of habit
- To avoid work
- To avoid writing
- To rubberstamp decisions.

As the chairperson has a major influence on the effectiveness and efficiency of meetings, you should, whenever possible, chair the meeting yourself. A small amount of time spent in preparation saves a great deal of time in the meeting. Make sure you allow time for the meeting preparation and treat it as seriously as being punctual for the actual meeting.

When chairing the meeting focus on ensuring its effective and efficient ending. Do not let any participant drift off the subject, reminisce about former times or do anything else that is not directly relevant to the topics under discussion.

The simple rules for effectively chairing a meeting are:

- Prepare before the meeting and read the papers.
- Prioritise the agenda items.
- Start and finish promptly.
- Be confident and stay in control of the meeting.
- Make it clear that the place for debate is at the meeting, and when a collective decision is reached, you expect it to be implemented, regardless of any individual's personal views.
- Let everyone have an equal opportunity to contribute and don't allow anyone (especially you) to dominate. (You know your opinions.)
- Listen, listen and listen.
- Summarise and ensure consensus, then move on.
- Vote only when it is clearly necessary.
- Ensure that the minutes reflect your recollection of the meeting.

You should build a reputation for running effective and efficient meetings.

ASSISTANTS

This is a trap for the unwary. You will need support in your role and most probably this will be in the form of a personal assistant (PA). Recruit the right person and you will be very happy; get this wrong and misery will ensue. Below are some tips to aid the recruitment of a PA.

You need someone:

- you can trust; their loyalty to you must be unquestionable;
- who is strong in your weak areas; if you can't spell, get a PA who can;
- who is extremely well organised;
- who will shield you from time wasters;
- who knows the company system;
- with a good personality (after all you will spend more waking time with your PA than with your life partner).

Be careful to remain the boss; do not allow back delegation to occur and do not accept sloppy work. Set high standards and keep your assistant busy, but also doing things that will help and evaluate performance at least quarterly. Do not wait if things are not satisfactory; this is a critical role and you must have the right support or your assistant may still be there long after you are not.

So, having mastered the reading, having control of the majority of your meetings, and having the right support, all you have to do is make things happen in accordance with the business plan and within the vision mission and values of the organisation for the benefit of the company, shareholders, employees, customers, creditors, fellow directors and the state.

THE MARKETING DIRECTOR'S PRIMARY AREAS OF RESPONSIBILITY

C4ISR is the military acronym for:

- Command
- Control

- Communications
- Computers
- Intelligence
- Surveillance
- Reconnaissance.

Command

In order to command you need to be able to issue instructions that are understood by those receiving them, and the recipients must have the will, capability, experience, training, equipment and opportunity to perform the tasks.

Many marketing directors give instructions without knowing if their employees have any of the necessary prerequisites to perform the task. Asking staff to organise a conference without ensuring that they know how to do it is clearly going to be a hit or miss affair.

With this in mind you will need to determine the capability of your teams. Answering these questions will help:

- What is the state of morale in the marketing function?
- What are our capabilities?
- What experience do we have?
- What training do we offer and does it meet our current and anticipated needs?
- What equipment do we have and what is its condition?
- What is our current level of staff utilisation?

Be cautious of the answers you get from the last question, and verify the responses objectively. No matter how overworked my team have claimed to be, they always managed to find the time to organise the company sponsored parties.

You will need to ask yourself: How good am I at giving instructions? The level of experience you will possess means that you are very likely to feel that every marketing task is very simple. You will long have forgotten what it is like for you to do that task for the first time. The sad reality is that your staff will have a mixture of intelligence and abilities. Some detail-oriented people will be essential in the implementation of projects, but they may feel lost when asked to view the "big picture". On the other hand, many visionaries do not pay sufficient attention to detail, and their implementation skills can be very poor as a result. Some people lack ambition; others are slow to learn and can easily forget that is why they are not the boss. So be sure you are communicating accurately to the level at which the action takes place. Take time to make instructions sufficiently detailed, and translate them accurately for the level and understanding of all staff that are required to act on them. Remember, if it can be misunderstood, it will be misunderstood. If it can be done wrongly, it will be; and if you think what's required is obvious, be prepared for a shock. Match your level of instructions to the ability and experience of those receiving them.

Control

Control is as important, if not more important, than command. If instructions have been misunderstood, you need to know about it sooner rather than later. Control provide us with the means of knowing that everything is going according to plan. There are many models that support control, from BS EN ISO 9001 systems to balanced scorecards and dashboards, all of which will be discussed in later chapters.

BS EN ISO 9001 and other quality initiatives

Whether its Six Sigma or any other quality initiative the basic idea is to document what you do and do what you say. What separates a hugely successful franchise operation from a "mum and dad" single outlet is systems that are documented, rigorously applied and tightly controlled.

Evaluation

In order to control you must measure and you should ensure that the company's marketing organisation is not only measured but regularly or, even better, continuously evaluated. The effectiveness can be measured by comparing actual performance against planned and benchmark standards such as: Product line profitability, market penetration, new-product/established product sales mix. Ensure that internal reports are maintained and that they provide adequate information on staff competences, key performance indicators (KPIs), and expenditure against budget. Ensure also that meeting assignments are being completed on schedule and that "early warning" control reports are on time, including Return on Investment (RoI) indicators.

If you use a quality system for work performance, make sure it is regularly and effectively audited. An annual external audit will not be effective in determining actual compliance, so your internal regular audits must be thorough. If there are no requests for changes, you may have a problem with your system, or it may only be getting lip service rather than being used. Quality systems are living, in that, they should change over time and encompass benefits of the learning curve and adoption of new methods and or technology.

If control is to be effective, you should maintain a list of pre-determined actions that must be implemented if performance is falling below expectations. You should also ensure that these directives are up to date and sufficiently clear to enable them to be actioned without delay when required. Clearly you cannot hope to cover every eventuality, but these predetermined action steps should cover the most likely scenarios.

Communications

We have already talked about the various public institutions and the need for effective communications with each of them. The primary system of communications outside the external marketing communications is probably going to be e-mail, web, telephone, meetings, face to face and mail. Some companies utilise net-meeting, web casts, blogs and even satellite communications. The new wave of web-based and Google-owned applications are generating new methods of communication and disseminating information. It is clear that the youth of today do not need, like the older generation, to print off documents in order to proofread them as they have acquired "on screen" checking skills. It is clear who we communicate with and how this is changing forever. So you should keep up to date with the latest developments and use whatever will enhance your communications process.

The latest generation of mobile devices means that you can receive e-mails on the road, take telephone calls worldwide, and access the Internet. These are essential tools for the marketing director, and cover telephone, video conferencing, messaging, e-mail, Internet and provide a power point reader, camera, video cam, etc. The cost of this technology will continue to fall and there is no real excuse for not having such basic tools. The features of the available communications technology changes month by month, but you need to enter at some point to benefit from this type of technology, even if it may be redundant 12 months later as new models arrive on the scene.

At one of the top French Business schools, HEC ESC in Paris, where I was attending an International Teachers Programme, one of the course delegates – a renowned businessman on the international stage – estimated that it took him about 12 hours to master a new program and its full functionality, and that unless you invested that time you would not get full benefit from the software.

This investment in time is more than returned in the speed and shortcuts you can then use regularly, so spend the time to learn how to use the technology to its fullest, especially the presentation software you rely on in your daily operations.

The wide availability and quick dissemination of videophone technology means that anything you say and do may be being recorded, so act accordingly. Do not exhibit any behaviour that your mother would not be proud to watch if you were on television.

A word of caution on communications, especially e-mail: As a board member anything you say has weight and authority, and e-mails can come back to haunt you or be used out of context. You therefore need to resist the temptation to fire off an immediate reply. As I have heard it said: Don't forget to engage your brain before opening your mouth, or responding to an e-mail. Take time to make considered responses.

The second biggest waste of your time is going to be the e-mail. Aside from the junk mail, your legitimate daily flow of e-mails can be highly disruptive to your day. Good time management means setting aside time to review e-mails, but not allowing other work to be displaced by low-priority but instant e-mail requests. Do what is urgent and important, and then what is important before what is only urgent. E-mails and telephone calls, because they are disruptive, have the appearance of being urgent but 80% of them will be quite unimportant. Don't be fooled into dealing with them and forgetting to do the non-urgent but important tasks on your desk. You need to use the technology; it should not use you.

Ensure you set the priority

A simple system I have found very effective over the years is to place work in three different coloured folders:

- *Red folders* for urgent and important work.
- *Blue folders* for important work that is not yet urgent.
- *Green folders* for everything else.

I then concentrate on the red folders first, then the blue, and if I have any time left I deal with the green folders. Very often the green folders are not actioned, and I have a clear out now and then, but at least I have noted or completed all the important items. I review the blue folders and upgrade them to red as they near their actionable date.

The major advantage to this colour-based system is that you can see at a glance any red folders on your desk, even in the middle of a stack of papers. My in-tray is also colour coordinated and I encourage staff to prioritise those items they want me to look at. I am also quick to reprimand an abuse of the system and in this way the staff have quickly learned not to put anything in a red folder that is not both urgent and important.

To get staff to understand how to prioritise, you will need to provide guidelines. I was able to do this by introducing a simple prioritising rule so that staff could judge the priority of work assigned to them. I assign tasks in a similar colour-coded manner and staff know what I feel is urgent and important. I do not confuse them by giving them tasks that have not been prioritised. With this very simple system there is no doubt about what I want done.

To help my staff to prioritise issues they give to me, I ask them to consider:

- Will it satisfy our customers?
- Is it profitable?
- Will it help the rate at which the company grows?
- Will it reduce our costs?

If it does any or all of the above, it's important and should be in a blue folder at least. If the opportunity is time critical and it satisfied the above, it's a red item. Everything else is green.

Computers

The role of marketing director today means having a complete understanding of how computers will aid your task. Consideration has to be given to access, security, software, data protection, as well as reliability and capacity.

Computers are used in almost every aspect of a modern business and marketing is no exception. It is imperative that marketing systems are integrated into the overall corporate computing model. As the primary source of revenue to the organization, marketing should be setting the agenda for the corporate computer requirements. If your CRM (Customer Relationship Management) system does not talk to your accounts system then you will find that you are selling to people who don't pay their bills, or are making sales calls on customers who have active open complaints, and this is hardly conducive to a successful sales visit.

If sales staff cannot access stock levels then they may sell things you don't have in stock or, worse, if stock/production systems are not available to sales they may turn away orders because they think items are not in stock or make unrealistic promises on delivery times.

Interoperability and effective integration should be a goal for every software item purchased. Therefore, you must consider software not only from a specific functional role or for the specific task it is required to perform, but also from the way it can be integrated into the overall computer environment. While the worldwide web and its associated computer languages are making this task easier to accommodate, care must be taken as far as possible to ensure compatibility between systems.

The main software tools required at the corporate level are data storage and retrieval systems, and above all the software must be resilient. On the hardware side the emphasis must be on high availability and therefore the systems need to have high reliability and be available when your team needs them. An acronym on the tie-pins of one of our early customers, (Tandem Computers, now part of HP) was YCDBWYCID. They sold at that time and HP still sell these "non-stop" highly reliable systems. The acronym stands for:

You Can't Do Business When Your Computer Is Down.

I recently called my insurance provider, "More Th>n", to be told to call back in a few hours as their system was down. I wonder how much business they lost during the time their computers were down. As computer failures can be catastrophic, make sure you agree with the Disaster Recovery Plan of the organisation. Ensure that it fits your sales team's needs and calculate the cost of the hours of downtime. Also ensure that the IT team have understood the impact of downtime on your area of responsibility. On the other hand, it probably did not lose "More Th>n" as much business as their call center, where the customer service representative could not understand English, especially in a Scottish accent, and the staff could not do anything that is not on their scripts! They certainly lost my business.

Tracking contract risk and obligations

Increasingly there are penalty clauses in purchase contracts; and while you should be familiar with your risk exposure, you must also ensure that you don't promise in the contract anything that you cannot deliver. A good tool is a "contracts risk calculator". This scans contracts and provides you with a list of the corporation's current contractual risk exposure.

A good starting point to get computing under control is a hardware and software audit. These can be run by a very clever piece of software that scans the entire network, so you should talk to the IT department about their utilisation. The audit provide you with a list of all the software and system hardware on the network, and from this list you can get a view of all the marketing software being used, its version, and the age and capability of the IT infrastructure being utilised by marketing staff. This is a great starting point and the audit will allow you to evaluate where you are and be an informed basis for the formulation of your vision of your desired marketing technology. The results of the marketing hardware and software audit may surprise you. You will almost certainly find that you are paying licence fees on software that no one is using, and that software that could help your team is not available on the corporate network.

Intelligence

Intelligence is the advantage you can generate from analysis and interpretation of information and data. Although there is no short-age of data, the problem is that most of it is not in a usable form. Intelligence is about sorting data, decoding it, analysing it, combining it, verifying it, interpreting it and using it to your organi-sation's advantage.

Intelligence, therefore, costs money and requires time to gen-erate, but it can make the company millions or it can be a complete waste of resource if it is not utilised before its "sell by" date. Like food, it is a perishable item – use it or lose it.

I have defined the intelligence process as follows. Some of these definitions may help, but as they are not uniformly accepted others may define them differently.

- *Data*: Individual facts/statements/opinions/lies; e.g. the price of a cup of coffee.
- *Information*: Data grouped, trended, sorted; e.g. a chart showing the price of a cup of coffee over time at a particular location.
- *Knowledge*: Information post-verification, analysis and human style interpretation; e.g. for the best quality, price and conve-nience buy your coffee at Fred's place.

- *Intelligence*: Knowledge that can be acted upon to the benefit of the organization; e.g. if we set up a coffee shop closer than Fred's with better quality at a lower price we can make a huge profit.

Reconnaissance

The Duke of Wellington said "time spent in reconnaissance is seldom wasted" and this is as equally true in business as it is in war.

Think of the choice of a retail site; you may have all the demographics of the area with overlays of purchasing behaviour, but nothing is better than walking the streets around the site, counting the foot traffic and getting a feel for the location and demographics.

Film-makers will send scouts to find locations before committing the film crew. In business, reconnaissance takes many forms but is a vital part of the marketing director's remit.

Surveillance

Bell Atlantic monitors its competitors' network coverage, as do many service providers, which is necessary for marketing planning and competitive opportunity. There is, however, a fine line between what is ethical and what is not. HP's board bugging of fellow directors' telephones was neither legal nor ethical surveillance in my view. The courts in the USA will have decided, by the time this book has been published, on the legal aspects but many shareholders already have, and resignations from the board suggest behaviour that was non-compatible with office.

INFORMATION AND ITS VALUE

Before we can offer information to others in the form of market intelligence we need to understand how others use information and what makes it actionable. What turns it into useful intelligence?

As important as the conduct of the research is the access to the research results and analysis. Flooding people with information is counter-productive while depriving them of it is equally bad. Have you ever been at a meeting where you have been annoyed at not being informed about something, only to be told that it was in such and such a report that you routinely receive?

Humans are animals that have survived by noticing differences in their environment. We can somehow block out the norm. Perhaps, our ancestors survived by noticing a movement in the bushes or an unfamiliar outline in the grass. This ability means that we tend to ignore, or not notice, our "familiar" environment after some time.

While working on projects in the hotel industry, I am often amazed how I can see so many things that are wrong, but those who work there day in and day out cannot. A classic example would be a worn carpet. Yes, they had noticed it but after a while they accepted it and no action was taken; meanwhile the image it was projecting to guests was costing the hotel money.

The art is to ensure that the right people get the right information at the right time. This of course is much easier said than done. Routine reports tend to be ignored if they are not completely relevant, while e-mail contains so much internally created junk that managers tend to ignore it too. As a marketing director intent on ensuring that the right information gets to the right people at the right time for them to take the appropriate action, you need a new approach to managing the flow of data throughout the organisation.

This new approach is called ENT, or Enterprise Neuron Trails. Like the human brain these trails, if activated, stimulate corporate memory and a response.

The ENT network is simply a map of the responsibilities of the managers and workforce. In all organisations there should be a reason for employing each person in the company. This reason is often documented in the job description, or KPIs (key performance indicators). By mapping job responsibility with information needs we generate an ENT for the organisation: a map of what people need to know to perform their role effectively and efficiently. It almost goes without saying that we can never be 100% certain of the information that staff need to do their jobs, but our goal, in the ENT, is to provide 80% of an individual's data requirements.

We can utilise the ENT to direct information or give access to those managers who are most likely to be interested in it and be able to act upon it. Having access is not in itself enough; managers need access at the right time, or when something has changed, and not necessarily when everything is normal or "as predicted". Currently some managers prefer to see even the "as predicted" result for fear that, if they don't get this information, things may be going wrong. In many organizations, you notice that things may be going wrong by the lack of information provided. "No news is NOT always good news."

As ENT's are established, there is a change in the information flows and more trust in information can be established. Remember, communication is a two-way process and therefore ENT is a two-way process. Where there is no feedback on the relevance of information or on how it is being used, the ENT system will tend to default to sending too much information and its value will diminish. Feedback raises the relevance of data provided, while no feedback will erode the 80% data relevance that we expected at the start of the exercise.

Information needs to be priority classified, and I recommend the use of the simple red, blue and green approach mentioned earlier. That is: information or market intelligence coded RED is both urgent and of importance to the recipient (sales are falling below estimate); BLUE is important but not urgent (sales are on target); and GREEN is information that the individuals can access when they choose to. Green presents the most challenge as it is difficult to predict what information an individual may require. For this reason web-accessible easily searchable knowledge databases are needed. By utilising these tools, staff can easily find what they are looking for after a little practice and appropriate training. The search engine and "all searchable" databases have benefits over traditional databases in that they do not require such a detailed save classification or such a strongly guarded filing policy. These "blogs"-style knowledge bases can be made to work very effectively. But please don't underestimate the need for effort in the establishment of these intranets because the knowledge tree created is only as strong as its weakest branches.

The aim of an ENT is to establish, in the longer term, not simply an information stream leaving it up to the individuals to turn that information into knowledge and intelligence, but a short-cut system that provides them with intelligence directly. This is a longer-term goal as individuals must share much of their time and knowledge to allow you to generate the processes that turn the information into useful intelligence quickly enough to be of use. The advantage of doing this is that, while perhaps only one person could previously interpret the data and gain intelligence from it, you would now be able to multiply the process, allowing the company to benefit by increasing the corporate knowledge base and, perhaps, providing that intelligence to less insightful staff who can nevertheless execute tasks that exploit the market intelligence or defend your market position.

KNOWLEDGE SECURITY

When you create a knowledge-base for your organisation the issue of security will be raised. This has to be addressed because a knowledge-base can only be effective if its knowledge can be accessed. The more restrictions placed on the access, the less effective is the knowledge-base, but there is also a lower risk of unauthorised use. Information has to be classified into categories relating to its sensitivity. Clearly, financial information in a public limited company must remain classified until such time as the public announcement is made to avoid the potential for insider trading, among other things.

The UK's Department of Trade and Industry recommends that information should be categorised into three levels: SEC 1, SEC 2 and SEC 3.

- *SEC 1*   Information that is private but not highly confidential. The majority of information (I estimate 60%) in a company knowledge base falls into this category.
- *SEC 2*   Information that could cause significant harm if disclosed. This will be about 30% of the information and includes all market intelligence.
- *SEC 3*   Information that would cause very serious damage if disclosed. This is very small proportion – probably less than 10%.

Who gets access to what is a matter for debate, but a policy is required that balances the risks of giving access to information and the loss of opportunity that results from restricting access.

Web or intranet access

Knowledge access is one of those 24/7 things. It should be available when and where staff members need to have access. Therefore, the only practical solution is a secure web access-based system.

Dynamic Insight

This type of system, e.g. GMAS by Marketing Management Services International Ltd, allows research results to be delivered securely and dynamically, so that users can request a certain survey, the period they want to check, and have the results generated in real time. From the broadest results overview, respondents can drill down to find out who gave a particular response to a particular question, at a particular time. The purpose of Dynamic Insight is that it gives an authorised user access to research being gathered in real-time at the right time in the right format for the user's purpose.

Competitive Intelligence Acquisition

Fredrick the Great wrote: "It is pardonable to be defeated, but never to be surprised." There are both moral and ethical issues to marketing intelligence and its acquisition for strategic planning, and, as HP found out recently, crossing the line can damage the company's image.

The principles of CIA

Competitive Intelligence Acquisition (CIA) is the process of acquiring data, testing or monitoring, sorting and processing, and determining what is useful and what is not. This is done in what is known as a STORM (Strategic, Tactical, Operational Review Meeting). Once the useful information has been extracted, it can be applied to provide a marketing advantage for your company.

What does CIA do?

Professor Bernard Jaworski of the University of Arizona reports that Competitive Intelligence leads to:

- Increased quality
- Improved strategic planning
- Superior knowledge of the market.

What else can CIA do?

CIA provides the ability to:

1. Effectively identify and anticipate changes in the market place.
2. Predict competitor actions.
3. Learn in advance about political, legislative or regulatory changes that affect your business.
4. Benchmark and improve your organisation's business practices.
5. Implement management systems and processes.
6. Provide a competitive advantage.

Why do organisations increasingly require competitive market intelligence?

1. The pace of business is increasing and the time available to make decisions is reducing.
2. Data overload is making it increasingly difficult for managers to find the time to analyse data, let alone extract useful information and apply it to the company's advantage.
3. Increased global competition means that competitors arise from anywhere.
4. Existing competitors are becoming more aggressive.
5. Political changes have a faster and more forceful impact than they once did.

6. Rapid technological change and the increased dangers of com-
    petitor breakthroughs can produce paradigm shifts and destroy
    your market in a very short space of time.

Why don't more organisations use CIA?

The regular reason that are given for not employing CIA
include:

1. We already "know the market" (I hope they are right!).
2. Nothing important happens outside our company as we "lead
    the world" (as did the American automotive industry until the
    Japanese taught them an expensive lesson).
3. Competitive Intelligence is "spying" (a misconception caused
    by confusion between gathering competitive intelligence and
    industrial espionage: one of which is legal and ethical, while
    the other is illegal and unethical).
4. Competitive Intelligence is "too costly" (if you think it is
    expensive, then count the cost of ignorance).
5. It has been tried before and it does not work (only recently
    has the technology to undertake effective CIA been available
    and the STORM concept to turn it into actionable
    knowledge).

MARKETING INTELLIGENCE

The gathering of competitive marketing intelligence can be divided
into six levels:

MI 1   Gathering secondary research on markets or competitors.
MI 2   Gathering primary research on markets or competitors.
MI 3   Undertaking private or public benchmarking with markets
       or competitors.

MI 4   Active intelligence gathering.

MI 5   Defence against industrial espionage.

The Legal and Ethical Line

MI 6   Offensive intelligence gathering, including infiltration and other forms of industrial espionage, which are best left to various state security services.

MI 1

This is standard practice performed in almost all firms when you look at the competitive market position, as reported by third parties.

MI 2

Most firms gather information during surveys to determine how their products or services compare to those of competitors.

MI 3

Many companies participate in the "benchmarking" exercise. For example, almost all the major oil firms participate in IT systems to benchmark activities for mutual benefit and reduce IT costs across the industry. MI-3 is very effective at taking costs out of the supply chain and in remodelling or re-engineering business processes, and it is normally mutually beneficial to all those that participate.

MI 4

This is active intelligence gathering, such as visiting a competitor and noting their prices or mystery shopping involving competitors' outlets.

In the telecommunications industry, Bell Atlantic and AT&T are both cited in recent literature as using active intelligence gathering. For example, Bell Atlantic physically monitors their competitors' mobile phone coverage while AT&T maintains a database of in-house experience/expertise that is utilised to provide added insight into research gathering.

MI 5

These are the steps you take to defend your company from industrial espionage. This can include such things as sweeping boardrooms for bugs, having scramblers on telephone lines and, most importantly, the defence of your computer systems from hackers.

MI 6

Rather like its namesake, Military Intelligence 6, this is the involvement in covert operations. Watergate is a prime example, but there are many others. Companies who undertake this type of activity are breaking the laws of most countries in the world. However, we have been a victim of this and perhaps you have been too. We once took on a trainee consultant, who was quite excellent and whizzed through our training programme, getting some of the top marks. This chap came in early, worked late and always wanted to do extra work. He kept great notes and copies of everything, building a portfolio, as he explained, "to help him do his job better". One day my secretary showed me a recovered document she had found when opening up her computer. The document was a half written note to one of our competitors thanking him for lunch and confirming that he would have the rest of the information by Friday. On checking the computer access records this chap had been systematically looking through all our knowledge base and copying files. I called him in and he resigned, but even then he tried to leave with some of our files which were only all returned after we made a threat of prosecution. I contacted the police, but they really did not want to know. We had been losing jobs to unknown competitors, which was found on many occasions to have been by the competitor this chap was obviously working for. No wonder he was so good! The damage was considerable and could have been disasterous for the company had it not been detected.

I subsequently discovered that this company had another great scam. It owned a temp agency, supplying secretaries, etc., and debriefing the temporary staff after each assignment. In this way they were able to identify the consultancy services they should promote to each company. Knowing the politics and the problems was worth a lot to this organisation.

This company failed, as the directors began to cheat each other, but they made a lot of money while they were in existence. I can't help thinking that if they had put half as much effort into legitimate business practices, how rich could they all have been by now?

Having irrefutable research is key to being successful in the market, and the methods of collecting the data, together with its accuracy, reliability and above all validity, are paramount.

SUMMARY

- Like the army general there are very similar activities that fall into the remit of the marketing director.
- There are systems and procedures to aid marketing directors do their job.
- Market Intelligence is fabricated from data, information and knowledge and is worthless unless you can take advantage of it in a timely manner.

We shall discuss C4ISR in more detail in the next chapter.

CHAPTER 4

MARKETING ADVANTAGE FROM TOP DOWN AND BOTTOM UP

I've got to follow them. I am their leader.

Alexandre Ledru-Rollin

LEADERSHIP AND LEADING BY EXAMPLE

At MMSI Ltd we have a policy on air travel which states that, when travelling with a client, consultants can travel in the same class as their clients but must otherwise travel economy class. It is essential that these rules are applied fairly and uniformally. If I were to travel first class, but expect my staff to travel economy class, I would build resentment and hugely increase our costs. It is important to be seen to comply with the rules, and to lead by example.

Leadership is the management process of coordinating three tasks: team building, individual team member development, and task achievement. One of the best writers on the subject is

Professor John Adair, and his website can be found at www. johnadair.co.uk.

In every task you set your teams, try to ensure that they not only achieve the task's successful completion but, in the process, build the team and develop the skills of the individual team members.

C4IRS

In the previous chapter we discussed the C4ISR role of the marketing director and in this chapter we will look specifically at the systems available to assist you in handling the C4ISR aspects of your company.

Computers

As the price of computer power, and especially memory, continues to fall the opportunity to use computers effectively throughout the organisation increases. The convergence of computers with telephones means that it is now difficult to determine where the boundaries are.

The recent generation of mobile phones, such as O_2's Xda range, offers a huge performance boost to productivity, allowing staff on the move to gain almost worldwide access to the internet and hence your corporate knowledge base. Orders can be taken, stock can be checked, discounts can be approved, etc., in real time almost anywhere.

The challenge facing the marketing director is knowing where the technology will add the highest value in the shortest period of time. The software and human interface is the real issue, in addition to how to get the technology adopted and its promise realised.

Millions have been spent on systems only to have them abandoned; it is only common sense to ensure that you can successfully handle the human side of technology introduction.

For example, the addition of a simple GPS application to your PDA or mobile phone can increase productivity by reducing the time sales staff take to get to their sales prospects. This translates into more calls and less missed or late shows at meetings. The software costs cost around £99 but by the time you read this book it will probably cost less. Is this a good investment?

Things to take into account:

- Cost of software
- Cost of hardware
- Cost of training in use or self-study
- Loss of sales during training (if training is not already budgeted for sales staff's time allocations)
- Number of sales staff
- Existing or new account balance (i.e. do you have a sales force of order-takers going to the same locations that they know very well, or is every call a first call to a new location?)
- Number of calls made per day
- Geographic dispersion of calls
- Size of order
- Alternative investment opportunities.

Whether the purchase is a good investment or not will depend on the above factors, but even something as apparently simple as spending £99 needs careful consideration, so take time to ensure that you don't promise something that you later have to refuse. It is very easy to feel that a program or a piece of hardware is going to solve a problem, but it often creates more problems and has a lot of hidden costs. I remember working for a company called Ascend Communications in Alemeda, California. We had been tasked with setting up a CPR (Customer Problem Resolution) team. Their job, for key accounts on a global basis, was to cut through the red tape and fix the problems for these very valuable customers. We decided we needed to install a group-based project management system and the one we recommended to do the job was e-mail based and very easy to use. It was a cheap and cheerful package costing around $500 for a five-user system. They had a small team at the time and our proposed system would have been adequate, as we could add users as the team grew. The software was required to run on the corporate network as it was not web based. The IT department wanted to conduct compatibility testing before they would allow the software on the system, and stated that a cross-department charge would be incurred. As they did not support the package, it would be necessary to have a help desk person trained to support the new system, assuming that it successfully passed the compatibility and non-conflict tests. The cost would be $50,000 and they were confident they could have the software installed and operational within six months! The staff of the IT department were on another planet.

It would have been cheaper and faster to install a complete new independent network for this team. This is how IT departments can lose the plot, why individual departments declare independence, and why we get lots of non-compatible systems and unauthorised software installed on networks.

A huge internal marketing job was required to remind the IT department that they were there to facilitate business, not block it.

It is the marketing director's job to ensure that everyone in the company, every department, and every function and cog in the organisational wheel, knows the importance of clients and that it is the customer's money that pays their wages. They would not be employed if there were no customers.

It is essential that you get the right computer support and the right attitude from the IT department, and it is important that IT has a unified strategy. The customers' needs and their time frames must always be considered and legacy systems must not be allowed to kill the company.

In many new areas of business, the older the company the less they are responsive because they are running legacy systems. New competitors enter with faster, cheaper, more user-friendly technology and rapidly steal their market share. Firms sometimes hold on to an obsolete system far too long on the basis that it is too costly to change. Well, from the marketing perspective, the reality is that it's often too costly *not* to change.

COMMUNICATIONS AND COMMAND

The line between communications and computing is very blurred and Voice-over Internet Protocol (VoIP) has brought communications to the computer systems while telephone systems have added computers to the hand-held telephone.

Here I have to draw a distinction between communications in the "telephone" sense and communications in the "meeting of minds" sense.

Communications is all about the meeting of minds, and therefore the message and the media have to be coded in such a way that the original meaning gets understood and acted upon by the recipient.

I must confess that this is not one of my strong points. I know what I mean to say, but somehow the urgency and the required actions do not get communicated properly and, hence, the task does not get done. I have then to suffer the consequences.

Let's spend a little time on this issue as it is, of all the skills, the one in which you will need a mastery to be absolutely proficient.

The first point to note is that staff do not like to be given orders to do something without a reason they can understand. The key word here is "understand". Most people would do something if they understood why you needed it done, but as we often do not have time to communicate well, we bypass the understanding stage and simply issue an instruction. In a time of crisis this is accepted by everyone, but outside of a crisis it is rarely effective in getting the job done exactly as you want it unless you are available for close supervision, which is not something a marketing director can afford the time to do.

The dilemma is, how much time do I take explaining what needs done over just doing the task myself. It is the old issue: do I teach a man to fish or simply give him a fish? It's quicker and easier to just give him a fish if it's a one-off request, but if he is going to come back time and time again, then it makes sense to teach him how to fish.

The other issue we often have is the physical lack of time to do all the one-off tasks required and we, therefore, have to trust others to do things that, perhaps, we feel we could have done better ourselves. Think of hiring a consultant. Most of the people who hire me are very experienced and could probably do the job themselves. However, they have assessed that they need someone else to do some of the jobs that they need done well but are not their top priority, or the task may be too "political" for them to simply do the job themselves and they need to be seen to use a third party to come to the same conclusion that they have already reached. At other times they just require an outsider's view or a particular skill set needs to be acquired.

Consultants on the whole do a good job and will earn their cost many times over in savings or increases in sales or profits, but before they can help you they need a brief, just as your staff do. The more detailed the brief, the better the response. You would never consider hiring an external consultant without providing him with a detailed brief, and for complex internal assignments you also need to provide a detailed brief. If a consultancy project is going to be effective it is imperative to have the client's feedback at regular intervals during the assignment, and, similarly, when assigning tasks we need to ensure that our staff get feedback and provide us with regular progress reports. At the end of a consultancy assignment the brief is compared to the results, and any modifications that were made during the assignment and the project are evaluated. Likewise, staff-assigned projects need regular feedback and results need to be assessed.

Delegation

As the marketing director you will be widely delegating your authority to ensure that all your objectives are achieved for the company. Delegation is not abdication of responsibility, and we have to know how to delegate tasks effectively and monitor progress towards a successful conclusion.

I have often got this wrong in the past, delegating tasks without expanding on the resources available or providing the minimum of information required – for example, by not providing a means of prioritising the many tasks being undertaken by people in the organisation or by not listening and confirming that the tasks are on track.

I would like to share with you simple system that I find useful; please feel free to adapt it and improve it. All I ask is: If you have an improvement, please let me know. The steps are as follows:

Define the task and set the priority. Determine the skills needed and ensure that they are held by the people being assigned the project. If they do not currently possess the skills needed, do they have the ability to acquire the skills and is sufficient time built into the project deadline to enable them to do so?

You have responsibility for the project because the above are your decisions. If you get it wrong, then you are to blame, not the people receiving the assignment. They are only *accountable*, you are *responsible*.

Having defined the project, set the priority, and assigned the staff members, the real communication challenge is ensuring that what you consider to be a successful outcome is also in the minds of the staff assigned.

Consider among your goals not just the task but also how the process of achieving the task will develop each individual team member as well as help to build a stronger team. The form below can help.

PROJECT BRIEF

Project/Task: (Enter Project Number & Name)
Priority level: (see Note 1)
Date: **Assigned by:**   **Assigned to:**

Objective/Desired

SMART Objective/shared vision/results not methods/describe the results. Be: Specific, Ensure results are Measurable, Achievable, Realistic and Time-framed.   Task: Individuals:

The Team:

Guidelines

Facts/information/suggested approach. (If you have done the task before explain how you did it but don't be too restrictive or prescriptive.)

Priority and Resources

> *Note 1* – Priority level: 1 = take action; 2 = take action but stay in touch; 3 = get approval before moving on; 4 = do only what I tell you to do.
>
> How much freedom
>
> State any limitations/budgets, etc.

Accountability

> Criteria: Measurable, observable, and discernible.
>
> How will it be followed up?
>
> How will performance be measured and evaluated.

Why and Consequences

> Describe what the project means to the company:

Date of Project Review Meetings/Project Completion Deadline/ Milestones

Report Back Immediately If:

> Describe any situations that you want immediate feedback on if encountered

If filling in the form was the only issue, then that would be fine, but it is imperative that you get the person/s receiving the assignment to feed back to you in their own words what they are being asked to do. (Similar to a consultancy assignment, you prepare a brief, to which the consultant responds in the form of a Terms of Reference or proposal.)

Having ensured that the assignment is understood it is imperative that you keep the scheduled review and milestone meeting and provide feedback on progress. A word of caution: do not accept a report that all is well, you must satisfy yourself of the task's progress by checking work to date, records of meetings, etc. – that is, make it a mini progress audit. I once lost a considerable amount of business by listening to what I wanted to hear from a senior consultant who, until we lost the business, assured me that all was well. The moral of the story is always check progress against measurable indicators assigning more of your attention to the project if all is not well.

CONTROL

Having sorted out your delegated projects it is now time to consider where you should concentrate your efforts within the company. In order to do this we need to have an aim or vision. The main aim of the marketing director may be to ensure that the company is in a position of leadership and power in its chosen market and to defend that position against the competition. Charles McDonald, in *The Marketing Audit Workbook*, wrote:

> Market leadership and marketing power are achieved only by firms in which the marketing function and its managers have enough influence and "clout" within the organisation that there is a strong marketing orientation throughout the company.
>
> . . . move your marketing function into a position of internal power and keep it there despite the well-intentioned efforts of your colleagues to make their functions dominant instead.

This is a view I share. Marketing must lead the organisation's vision and command the board's attention, above all other functions, if the organisation is to prosper in the ever-increasingly competitive world markets.

Balanced scorecard

The Balanced Scorecard approach, developed by Kaplan and Norton, has been widely adopted by many of the world's largest companies, and software to support its deployment has been developed by some of the world's leading names in the software industry. It is an excellent system that helps you to focus on areas that require your attention.

The model featured in Figure 4.1 involves the strategy being viewed from four different perspectives; namely, the financial, the customer, the internal and learning and growth.

(a) The financial view

The ultimate objective of this view is to "improve shareholder value". Improved shareholder value comes as a consequence of the offsetting of income growth against increased productivity within the company. The factors of income growth and productivity both consist of two main subsections. Within income growth, the contributing factors are the expansion of the market and the increase of income from the present client base. The two factors that lead to increased productivity are increased efficiency and better use of current resources, combined with large investments being replaced by gradual investments.

You will see quite clearly that as the marketing director you have a role to play in all these areas, starting with shareholder value. From the marketing perspective, we need to apply to shareholder value, the same activities and actions that we undertake to

The Strategy Map Describes the Strategy
Case: Hi-Tech Strategy Map

Figure 4.1 Strategy views. (Copyright 2001 Balanced Scorecard Collaborative, Inc. • Gscol.com. Reproduced with permission)

ensure customer value. Value is made up of two elements: real value and perceived value.

Real value

What the investment is really worth is based on the assets, current profits, and the accountancy based "factual" data. However, this is rarely used in isolation to value a company's shares. The older mature industries measure a higher proportion of their value on the basis of real value, while this form of measurement is less used in new businesses as the balance sheet (real value) often does not support the share price.

Perceived value

This is the premium or discount associated with the real value and takes account of the markets expectations. Investors consider the company's future earnings potential, the CEO's and the management team's track record, company regulations, competition, market potential size, and a whole host of future factors. This perceived value is what creates the volatility in markets. All shareholders or perspective shareholders do not perceive the same value in the shares. Where they perceive a bargain they buy in, where they perceive an over-valuation they bail out, and take the profit or accept the loss. This is what creates the super companies that are valued at many times more than their balance sheet value, e.g. Google and most of the other internet-based firms. I call these "faith" valuations. The market has faith that the company will, in the future, deliver what it expects. It is interesting to note that the market often exceeds the faith the management have in their own company. For example, the CEO of Cisco Systems has year on year played down the stock to try to keep investors' expectations within the company's ability to deliver. In other companies, where the market has been allowed to hype the stock, they will at some point fail to deliver and the share price will crash.

The ability of the company to deliver value to shareholders is therefore not simply an accounting function but a marketing or de-marketing function. As the marketing director represents the highest authority within the company on marketing, it is imperative that those skills are also applied to shareholder perceived value management.

Some companies give shareholders discount vouchers on the firm's merchandise or services, increasing perceived shareholder value, while others encourage staff and suppliers to be shareholders.

Clearly the marketing function has a major role to play in revenue growth and can also influence productivity. The size of order, the style of packaging, etc., all impact on productivity, and as special orders can be much more demanding to produce than standard orders, it may make sense to support productivity by targeting particular types of sale or limiting product design to existing dimensions.

(b) The customer view

Kaplan and Norton describe this section as "the heart of the strategy". This area outlines the exact strategy for gaining new custom or for enlarging the current customers' division of business. This is clearly an area for the marketing director's input and contribution.

(c) The internal view

This view outlines the corporate processes and exact action that a company must perfect in order to maintain the customer view, which, as has already been said, is fundamental to the success of the company. The marketing director again has a key role to play in this area.

Learning and growth view

Kaplan and Norton outline the 'unquantifiable' resources that are necessary to allow the goals of organisational actions and client/ company interaction to be carried out at increasingly sophisticated levels. There are three main sections to be considered within the learning and growth view. The first is that of strategic capabilities. This section encapsulates the knowledge and abilities demanded from the staff in order to maintain the strategy. The second section is that of "strategic technologies" (Norton & Kaplan, 2001: 93). This part is concerned with the technological requirements that are necessary to maintain the strategy. The third and final area that contributes to the learning and growth view, is the environment for activity. Within this part the effect of shifts in the social atmosphere of the organisation are taken into account as the optimum environment in which to maintain the strategy is examined. The marketing director has a role here and specifically in the partnering with customers.

The marketing director's role in the development and success or otherwise of a balanced scorecard implementation is one of the most important as the balanced scorecard is a very customer-focused model. You can add to the balanced scorecard to ensure that the reality of market, as well as the ability to detect and respond to operational execution errors, are evaluated. The risk in a company using a Balanced Scorecard system can therefore be substantially reduced.

INTELLIGENCE

In the previous chapter I mentioned the process of taking data through information to knowledge and on to intelligence. We will now look at how this is done in reality.

Rather like in all marketing activity we start with the customers and their existing needs. We then move on to the "arts marketing model" and develop their future needs from that perspective. Let's look at the questions we need to answer:

- What data, information, knowledge and intelligence (DIKI) are currently needed in order for the organisation to function effectively?
- What DIKI is gathered and by whom for what purpose?
- Stop disseminating DIKI that is not used. Did anyone scream? Add back only the DIKI that is needed to stop the screams.
- Benchmark our effectiveness. If we are not close to the top of the list, what DIKI do others use to be more successful than we are?

- Match that DIKI and disseminate note impact on benchmark position.
- Write an analysis of how best to do the jobs you are currently doing. What DIKI would be needed to beat the competition?
- Can you ethically and realistically gather the DIKI required?

In this process you will find that there are problems within your organisation with the compatibility of data. Some common issues are:

- The CRM (Customer Relationship Management) system does not interact with the accounting system.
- Data on some customers is not available to other departments.
- Data protection issues have not been resolved and you are not getting the right permissions on data capture to suit the data used elsewhere in the company.
- Data can be unreliable; there can be double counting, data entry error, incomplete records and even fraudulent information.

The most important aspect of data is that it must be reliable. I use a 3F model to explain DIKI: It is all made up of Fact, Faith and Fiction.

All DIKI contains a mixture of fact, faith and potential fiction. For example, we know when the company was registered (Fact); we have projections and budgets that we will use to build our business and these are based, one hopes, a sound understanding of the market and our cost structure (Faith); when we begin to execute the plan, where we end up may not be where we intended, and therefore the plan has the potential to contain spurious information (Fiction).

The majority of large company initiatives fail to start on schedule and to complete on time. This is surprising considering the experience of most companies involved in major initiatives. Based on a study of large US organisations, Bain & Co., the strategic consultants, reported that at any one time as many as 11 major management approaches can be in implementation within the same company.

This is almost like MBBS (Management By Best Seller) where management simply introduces the approach suggested by whichever book happens to be the best seller in that quarter. This constant change has created, in most companies, a feeling of apathy towards new initiatives. This must be overcome if the synergies and benefits from the various management approaches are to be gained, or the alignment behind one approach is to be achieved.

Being able to distinguish between fact, faith and fiction is critical for the successful implementation of any plan. As soon as fiction becomes apparent, action must be considered.

If, for example, we are in the CRM software business and we have assumed that the CRM market will continue to grow at 40% per annum over the next 2 years, our strategy will be impacted if it comes to light that the market is growing by less than that amount. Sales, manufacturing capacity, inventory, etc., will all be affected.

Looking through all the DIKI we establish that the critical assumption upon which most of the planning is based is the information that the market is growing at 40%. As it is so critical it is only prudent to verify the information. On further investigation you find it to be a widely reported figure in the media, but the source is not provided in the majority of cases. In those cases where it is reported, it is described as being from trade sources or Siebel Systems.

As Siebel was the market leader at the time (now part of Oracle), they may have had a vested interest in reporting a rapidly growing market. Alarm bells should be starting to ring, and this should trigger primary research. You need to know the growth rate in the market. Primary research reveals a growth rate of only

20% based upon growth in sales of CRM companies and a market study.

Determine the Fact and be alert to Faith and Fiction. Siebel believed the market would grow at 40% and the press reported the high number, not as an optimistic forecast but as a fact. Other media subsequently used this and before long it was accepted as market knowledge. In a corporate intelligence system this should never have gone further than information. To become intelligence it has to have been verified.

There will be more later on how to separate Fact, Faith and Fiction.

SURVEILLANCE

Surveillance in the context of business is not so much spying as monitoring things in real time. In the previous example we determined that a critical success factor was the market growth rate. As it was so critical to our success, it would warrant close surveillance. In other words, a one-off study to determine the growth rate would simply not suffice and a real-time monitoring methodology would be required such as a weekly or monthly benchmark or a continuous research study. Clearly the importance of the critical success factor and its time dependence will have to be considered against the cost of surveillance. In the majority of cases surveillance is limited to customer satisfaction, customer complaints monitoring, etc. The actual balanced scored screens that many firms now employ show the critical success factors, and the data used to generate them originates from real-time or near real-time systems. These systems need to be protected from fiction and should be strongly fact based.

Real-time right-time systems such as Dynamic Insight (Figure 4.2) from MMSI Ltd provide a balanced scorecard type screen outlining the position of the company in relation to its customer

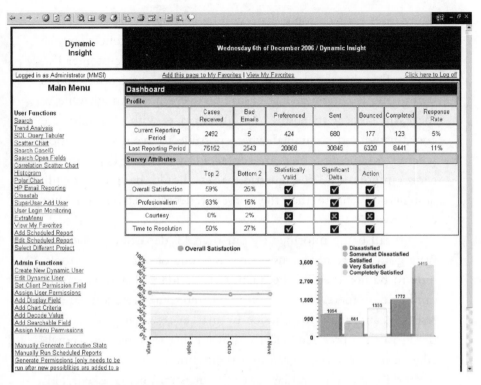

Figure 4.2 Screenshot of Dynamic Insight

satisfaction objectives and how those impact on competitors' customer satisfaction.

RECONNAISSANCE

This can be translated into market research. It is only prudent before any major investment for research to be conducted into the market and for the lay of the competitive landscape to be determined.

When you examine the company you will not be surprised to find all sorts of research being conducted by almost every department. What will surprise you is the lack of coordination and in many cases your customer base will be getting contacted to complete several studies from different departments. For one client we were asked to undertake a study and were given a customer list, only to find that the same list had been used for three other studies within the last month. The customers were not amused. One of the early tasks is to ensure that all contacts with customers are coordinated and combined where possible to avoid the situation where the same customers are contacted by different departments. More importantly, the questionnaires should be professionally designed to ensure that the survey reflects positively on your company.

I recall being informed by our own IT department that they were going to conduct a user-survey of one of our software tools, only to be horrified by the quality of the items that were sent to our key customers. Despite having written some great software for research, and being surrounded by market research professionals, the form they produced clearly showed that they had no knowledge of how to write a professional questionnaire. Everything was wrong, from design and layout to the questions being asked. This would NOT really have filled our customers full of confidence in our research ability! It is essential that you take charge of the external communications and ensure that all research activity is coordinated through your department, and don't take it for granted that other departments know about good marketing practices.

Having looked at the C4ISR model we can now turn our attention to several others that will make managing the role of marketing director a little bit easier.

MCKINSEY'S 7-S MODEL

One of the most useful models is McKinsey's 7-S (Figure 4.3). The McKinsey 7-S model is an effective aid to understanding the factors that make up an organisation, how they interact and how

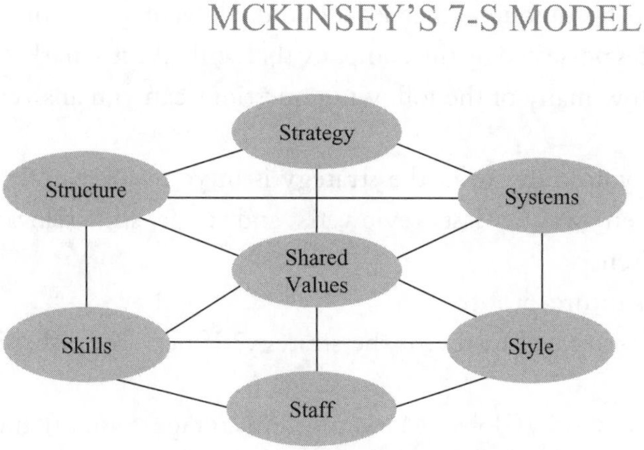

MCKINSEY'S 7-S MODEL

Figure 4.3 McKinsey's 7-S model. (Copyright 1979 McKinsey & Company. Reproduced with permission)

changing one element has a knock-on effect on all the others. The model was first devised as a means of comparing companies, and this is where its strength lies. (See the Glossary of Marketing Terms at the end of this book for a description of the model.)

Looking at each element in turn we can see that a company can be described in terms of:

- Strategy
- Systems
- Structure
- Skills
- Style
- Staff
- Shared values.

Strategy

This is the documented means by which the company will strive to have a competitive advantage over its competitors. Most strategies strive to be unique – that is, they take advantage of any unique attributes possessed by the company that will give it a market advantage. How many of the following questions can you answer?

- Do you know what the strategy is in your company?
- When was it last reviewed, and is it still relevant and current?
- Is it future-proof?
- Do you need to revisit the strategy? If not now, when?

In the GMAS (Global Marketing Advantage System) model of strategy developed around the STORM (Strategic, Tactical. Operational, Review, Management) model, strategy is only reviewed when it is challenged by non-achievement of objectives or when the critical assumptions on which it is based are compromised.

Systems

Whether these are based around ISO 9001 or any other standard, are these systems up to the task of managing the company's operations in the current and future market conditions? Many companies have failed because they have applied old systems in changed times, only to find that they are not suitable for the task.

Systems should be living, changing and evolving, but should not be diluted intentionally. Dilution occurs through ineffective training and needs to be especially guarded against in organisations using mentoring rather than formal training as their principal means of disseminating system knowledge. As a rule, the first person trained remembers 50% of the training – and mainly those items with which they are involved day to day. During their mentoring of others, they pass on 80% of the day-to-day know-how and only 30% of the background knowledge. After several iterations very little of the knowledge behind the system is understood, but the system may still be functioning. Those bits that did not appear immediately relevant have long been discarded. Gradually a well-tuned system, which delivered exactly what the customer wants, increasingly fails to deliver and often becomes the excuse for not delivering what the customer really needs. The knowledge of how the system was developed has long been lost, as are the implications of making any changes. In the worst cases the systems fail to deliver the critical success factors, and the company gradually or dramatically fails.

Structure

Every company has some form of structure, from a loose matrix management style to a militaristic chain of command. The structure has evolved over time and you will again have to determine if it is still suitable for your market.

Skills

What talents are there within the organisation? Are they individual knowledge based or corporate knowledge based? That is to say, if an individual was to leave would the company's ability to do the job be under stress? In many organisations many generations of cutbacks and not training apprentices has meant that knowledge has become concentrated in a few individuals who, as demographics have it, will be nearing retirement age. What is the situation in your organisation?

Style

Style refers to the manner in which the firm operates. There are many firms – e.g. Apple, Hewlett Packard, Goldman Sachs, Linklaters – that have a corporate style that sets them apart from others and can be a great draw to clients as well as prospective staff.

Staff

First-rate people hire first-rate people; second-rate people hire third-rate people.

Leo Rosen

How staff are recruited, their backgrounds, diversity and education all play a vital part in defining who the staff are and how they interact on and off the pitch.

Shared values

All the above combine with the organisation's vision and mission to generate a shared value system to which the staff all subscribe. This may or may not coincide with the stated values of the company. I have come across many firms where the staff values were clearly not aligned with the officially stated corporate values.

ALL TOGETHER

As you will have gathered, these items are not isolated. Making a change to one will impact all the others, therefore it is not something you want to do without having thought it through properly, and I am speaking from experience.

My own experience of failing to consider the model

Many years ago I had what I thought was a straightforward task to perform. It involved a simple change of one of our firms from a Limited Liability Company to a Public Limited Liability Company as a prerequisite to floating the company. I found myself caught up in a major change process instead of the simple change in name and a few more accountancy reporting requirements that I had imagined the process would involve. Owing to the new legal reporting requirements, I was inadvertently upsetting the style and structure of the company. This had knock-on effects in the skills required, staff attitudes and systems, and produced a major misalignment in shared values within the company almost overnight, which resulted in staff changes and loyalty being tested to the limit. This relatively minor change had major consequences that resulted in the delay and, later, cancellation of its flotation.

THE OPEN MIND

Having an open mind is essential for being an effective marketing director, as is an astute situational awareness, an ability to identify and understand patterns in data, and an aptitude for creativity.

These are quite distinct traits that aren't naturally associated. If the old stereotypes are to be given credence, creative people cannot be analytical and analytical types cannot be creative. There are some interesting companies that have exploited this niche offering courses for business analysts on how to be more creative and for creative people on how to be more business-like. These two activities, often referred to as right (creative) and left (analytical) brain activities, can be developed and right-brain-dominated individuals can find that by becoming good at left-brain activities they enhance their right-brain skills and vice versa. Tony Buzan and Edward De Bono provide a wealth of literature on how the mind works and on how to benefit from whole brain thinking. Anecdotal evidence suggests that some of the best minds in history have excelled in more than one discipline. For example; such notable figures as Leonardo de Vinci and Albert Einstein both excelled in creative and analytical activities.

With an increasing need to understand patterns in information and gain meaning from multiple sources – often containing conflicting data – it is not surprising that software tools have been developed to make this activity easier.

Below I have listed the top 50 excuses you will have to contend with from others when you try to have your new ideas accepted. I often put them on a slide at the start of a meeting – especially if I anticipate a hostile reception – in an attempt to prevent them from being used, with the note that these excuses are not being accepted today!

1. We tried that before.
2. My mind is made up, don't confuse me with facts.
3. We don't have the time.
4. Leave it until we are not so busy.
5. We have never done that before.
6. You will never get this through the finance committee.
7. We don't have the authority.
8. The members/shareholders will never accept it.
9. We are not against change provided it involves no alterations.
10. This is not our current policy.
11. We are not ready for that type of change yet.
12. It will run up the overheads.
13. We would be laughed at.
14. Far too academic/Ivory Tower.
15. We will lose many in the long run.
16. Let's get back to reality.
17. We do all right without it.
18. That is not our problem.
19. Where did that idea get dug up from?
20. Why change? Everything's working fine.
21. Our company is different.
22. I did not think of it so I don't like the idea.
23. Our company is too small.
24. You are right BUT!
25. It will cost too much.

26. You can't teach old dogs new tricks.
27. It's too big a risk.
28. Impractical.
29. It's never been tried before.
30. Let's hold it in abeyance.
31. It will not work here.
32. Let's give it more thought at another meeting.
33. It will make equipment obsolete.
34. Not that old chestnut.
35. It cannot be done.
36. We will need a detailed written report on the implications.
37. It's too much trouble to change now.
38. That may have worked in another company but it will not work here.
39. It will not pay for itself.
40. I'm not convinced.
41. Let's form a committee to discuss it.
42. Let's sleep on it.
43. The public will not like it.
44. Think of the disruption it will cause.
45. Has anyone else tried it?
46. I know someone who tried that and …
47. We are all far too busy to do that.
48. It has always been done this way.
49. Are you trying to teach me my job?
50. If it's so good, why have I never heard of it?

See how many you can come across and if you hear of others, please e-mail them to me at Gerald@marketingms.com.

BREAKTHROUGH MARKETING

Breakthrough marketing was developed from the work of Gerald Nadler and Shozo Hibino who described in their book a concept entitled "Breakthrough Thinking". This is a complex but highly rewarding read.

Their model provides a methodology with which multiple stakeholder groups can effectively address intricate problems or issues. By following the process, breakthroughs can, quite literally, be achieved in what at first appear to be non-solvable problems.

Nadler and Hibino present seven principles that provide a practical framework that can be employed to solve complex issues. As production of an effective strategy for a large or growing company in a turbulent, ever-changing market is a complex issue, the theory and practices recommended by Nadler and Hibino have been adopted into breakthrough marketing.

"Breakthrough marketing planning" comprises the seven principles of breakthrough thinking applied to marketing problem solution. As I mentioned previously, breakthrough-thinking principles were developed by Gerald Nadler of the University of Southern California, and Shozo Hibino of Chukyo University in Japan.

Breakthrough marketing planning is about the provision of marketing solutions that don't just match the competition, but blows it away. In most wars the availability of a breakthrough weapon was what really achieved the victory – for example, the long bow, the tank, the atom bomb.

The seven principles

- Uniqueness
- Purposes
- Solution after next
- Systems
- Needed information collection
- People design
- Betterment timeline

Uniqueness

Every business and marketing problem is unique, regardless of any apparent similarities. As such, each requires an initial approach that dwells on its unique contextual needs. Solutions from elsewhere should only be used if the context shows that it is appropriate. Copying others rarely provides a breakthrough.

Purposes

Unless you are sure and can agree on the purpose, little progress can be made in finding a lasting solution to the marketing challenge. Purposes can be viewed as a spectrum focusing in on the part that can be achieved, while leading on to a greater purpose can be determined by continually using the question of "why"? This process allows clear focus on the real purpose and strips away the non-essential, which so often slows up project completion or confuses priorities. As everyone in the same company will have a high degree of purpose overlap, it is your task to show the extent of the overlap and thereby demonstrate how it is in everyone's interest to work together, at least to some extent.

Solution after next

By accepting purpose as a spectrum, whatever we do to solve the current challenge will affect the future and should be considered as a stepping-stone rather than a barrier. Consideration to the future solutions and innovations is achieved easiest by working backwards from the future purpose. For example, building a flexible production line to ease future model modifications may be a better solution than building a rigged production system. Although, in the short term, costs may be less in the rigged system, knowing our future purposes will help us to make better decisions today that may work out better in the longer term.

Systems

Any marketing solution will affect the rest of the organisation and its effects should be calculated and implications assessed. Sometimes the less obvious implications are often the most critical, so ample time should be given to exploring the consequences of implementing any solutions that are derived.

When building a system around your solution, it should be your aim to de-skill 80% of the associated tasks and make them routine. Only when a system is in place delivering consistent results can quality improvements be effectively introduced. The remaining 20% deals with the non-standard solutions, and very few systems can predict the demands this 20% makes. Therefore, the cost–benefit analysis of building a system capable of handling 100% of situations often does not warrant its introduction, at least in the early development stages.

Needed information collection

We live in the information age – data is not in short supply. The problem is effectively mining the right information from the vast assortments of information that are available today. Clear purposes make the gathering of information much easier, as only information that will help to achieve the focused purpose should be gathered. There is a real danger today of information overload, which can be almost as dangerous as not gathering data at all.

People design

All those who are involved in the success of the implementation of a marketing solution should have been given the opportunity to contribute to the solutions being proposed. Only when those involved in the implementation have "bought into the solution" will the solution be effective. Many projects have failed because of sabotage, which has resulted from the actions of those who felt that a solution was being forced upon them and of which they felt no part.

Betterment timeline

Nothing lasts forever and no system will last forever. Therefore, solutions should be regularly reviewed in the light of the focused purposes and these review dates should be built into the system. A process of continual improvement should be introduced and policed as the future achievement of purposes means building systems that will grow and adapt to the changing market environment while remaining focused on the purpose for which they were designed.

This set of rules allows planning to be more effective and can be adopted today with quite remarkable positive effects.

The Japanese model for the introduction of new products

The Japanese model used to introduce new products takes about the same total time as in the traditional Western models, with much the same issues arising. The difference is that in the Japanese process there is much more consultation, discussion and scenario testing. In all, about 80% of the time spent in this planning phase is hidden from the glare of the open market compared to 20% of the time spent in planning in the typical Western model.

In the Japanese model the remaining 20% of the time will be spent dealing with the inevitable problems that arise in the early introductory phase of a new product (80% planning, 20% fire-fighting). This compares with the typical Western model where spending only 20% of the time on planning results in the need to spend 80% of the time on unscheduled fire-fighting (20% planning, 80% fire-fighting). High profile fire-fighting in full view of the public can damage the company image and consumer confidence in the company.

You should support the Japanese model, which maintains that 80% of any process should be completed prior to full market exposure, thus minimising the fire-fighting that is required to ensure a successful launch. This gives weight to the old adage of the 5 P's: Poor Planning leads to Pretty Poor Performance *or* Pre-Planning leads to Pretty Pukka Performance.

Take time to plan, and implementation goes faster with fewer problems.

Applying the breakthrough marketing model

- Identify as many purposes for the assignment as possible.
- Expand the purposes from those small in scope to those with the largest scope, placing them in a hierarchy, then, most importantly, select the purpose of the focus. Be "SMART" about this, i.e. state the purpose as you would an objective. That is, be S – specific, make it M – measurable, A – achievable, R – realistic and T – timed.
- Generate as many "solutions after next" until you see the achievement of the focused purpose. Each solution should be "SMART", then group these alternative options.
- Design systems that will be capable of handling 80% of things (the regular conditions) – don't try to build systems to accommodate everything, it's impossible. This will determine your "solution after next" target.
- Involve those who will be responsible for designing and implementing the solution. Take full account of their input and solve problems that they perceive may ensue from the solution models proposed.

- Gather only the information you need to develop the systems and ensure their successful implementation.
- Develop the recommended marketing solution that stays close to the target, but consider how the 20% of irregular conditions will be handled.
- Detail the recommended solution and pilot it, if possible.
- Design the project plan, including installation and transitions between the steps to achieve the purpose.
- Implement the plan, project, manage and trouble shoot.
- Set dates for betterment to attain larger purposes and parts of the target or to redesign the target.

Breakthrough marketing planning is an extremely useful tool in determining strategy and in the preparation of revolutionary plans. It allows for great creativity, but focuses the energy of the team towards a clear purpose. If applied, it will be responsible for more breakthroughs than almost any other single theory. It is what marketing has lacked in recent years. As a problem solver, it will allow clearer thinking, allow more effective solutions to be found, and enable more efficient implementations of those solutions, with less unforeseen problems arising.

SUMMARY

- Marketing-led companies have the greatest success.
- Marketing has a finger in every pie in the company, and so it should.
- Perhaps the most useful model for a new marketing director is the breakthrough marketing model which, if applied correctly, can move mountains.

The quality and reliability of DIKI will be discussed in the next chapter.

CHAPTER 5

CORPORATE GOVERNANCE AND RISK ASSESSMENT

Risk comes from not knowing what you are doing

Warren Buffett

You will recall that I mentioned corporate governance in the first chapter and expanded upon it in the second. It is now time to review what it means in practice to be a public listed company.

The first obvious question is: What is corporate governance? There are many definitions, ranging from "the effective management of the company" to "compliance with complex external governance principles". For many smaller companies there is no need to take the definition much further than effective management because the directors are, by and large, the shareholders and therefore the shareholders' and the directors' interests can be considered to be aligned. In public limited companies the shareholders are often quite removed from the company and a wider definition is required, such as that put forward in 1999 by J. Wolfensohn, the then President of the World Bank: "promoting corporate fairness, transparency and accountability". Others have gone further, encapsulating compliance with rules, processes, and laws in which the business operates, and by which it is regulated and controlled.

All the grand definitions focus on two distinct elements: internal control and external compliance. They are propositioned around the shareholders, the board of directors, management and the external government's representatives, the auditors.

Murray Steele of Cranfield University, reporting on the 1995 Greenbury report on Corporate Governance, divided the topic into 11 areas:

- Board performance
- Remuneration
- Training
- Disclosure of information
- Role of the audit committee
- Role of the nominations committee
- Conduct of the Annual General Meeting (AGM)
- Role of the chairman
- Role of the chief executive
- Role of the remunerations committee
- Directors' contracts.

This report and others, notably the Cadbury report of 1992, were the catalysts for the Financial Reporting Committee's (FRC) Code of Conduct. These were augmented after the Enron and WorldCom scandals in the USA. The most recent edition of the FRC's Code of Conduct can be found at www.frc.org.uk.

THE FRC CODE OF CONDUCT

The voluntary Code of Conduct sets out good practice in corporate governance. I have taken the main points from the Financial

Reporting Council's document *The UK Approach to Corporate Governance*, November 2006.

A single board should collectively be responsible for the success of the company, with:

- Separate chief executive and chairman
- A balance of executive and independent non-executive directors
- Strong independent audit and remunerations committee
- Annual evaluation by the board of its performance.

Emphasis should be placed upon:

- Objectivity of directors in the interest of the company
- Transparency on appointment and remuneration
- Effective rights for shareholders.

This is a voluntary code and is applied on the basis of "comply or explain". The FRC claims that this provides the "high standards of corporate governance with relatively low associated costs".

The European Corporate Governance Institute

To find similar Codes of Conduct for 64 other regions and countries, visit www.ecgi.org. You will also find there some American and European Codes of Conduct, all of which pursue a similar goal.

WHAT'S IT ALL WORTH?

So what is all the governance and compliance worth? *The McKinsey Quarterly* in 1996, Q4, reported that companies with good corporate governance enjoyed an 11% bonus on corporate value. Well, if true, this is a reasonable return on the investment. I feel by now that it is simply a cost of doing business and non-compliant companies are penalised by being slightly less attractive to investors. That said, investor greed can outdo investor caution, and some companies are still far from being compliant but enjoy high market valuations.

DOES ANYONE COMPLY?

The reality of the "comply or explain" option has resulted in more explanations than compliance. Each year Grant Thornton research compliance and in December 2006 they published the *Corporate Governance Review 2006* (see Appendix 3).

This review makes interesting reading, as only 31 companies said they were fully compliant, with the remaining 90% of respondents falling short of full compliance. This was broken down as follows, based on those claiming full compliance:

FTSE 350	34.1%
FTSE 100	42.9%
Mid 250	30.1%

This might at first sight be alarming reading, but when explanations are considered we find that some 96% of companies provide at least some reason for non-compliance. Thus, it could be argued that 96% of firms are working within the spirit of the FSC Code of Conduct and, to be fair, changes were only introduced as recently as June 2006. What is clear is that global institutional investors are expecting greater efforts at compliance and, on the whole, compliance will become more important to their investment decisions over the next three years.

It is only sensible for any new director to be aware of the current Code of Conduct. The current version can be found at www.fsc.org.uk. Ensuring that your organisation complies is going to become more important and will be an important factor in getting the support of institutional investors in the future. Early adaptors can take advantage of compliance to strengthen their appeal to institutional investors in the short term.

RISK

From the marketing director's point of view, and of particular significance, is the identification and quantification of risk. In many businesses it is market risk that is a significant factor, together with the cyclical nature of markets or the propensity for paradigm shift.

Marketing systems such as GMAS (Global Marketing Advantage System) provide a means by which firms can determine their exposure to market risk and paradigm shift and, therefore, provide quantifiable risk profiles for the organisation. In the Grant Thornton study only 56.4% of FTSE 350, and 47.2% of Mid 250 firms were compliant with the Corporate Governance Code of Conduct in this regard to measurement and quantification of risk compared with 76.5% of FTSE 100 companies.

There are several specific marketing risks, e.g. as the old advertising adage goes, 50% of our advertising is wasted but we don't know which 50%. Clearly there is a major risk associated with marketing campaigns and past history is no indication of future success. This risk has to be qualified and mitigated against. In the preparation of marketing action plans aimed at being implemented by clients, I opt for a triple redundancy approach. That means that if the action plan is completely and competently implemented in full, it would bring three times the expected results. In this way I can be sure that it contains enough fat to achieve the stated marketing objectives, and there are an adequate number of other options that can be implemented if any one particular activity fails to achieve its targets for any reason. This is a way of mitigating the risk of failure of a poorly implemented action, or just plain bad luck.

Another risk factor is that there are several reasons why past marketing performance may not be a good indicator of future success. A promotion can be effective one year and not the next for a number of reasons, ranging from media clutter to competitor action. These are risks that the marketing function is in the best position to recognise and quantify, while other risks may be present in the product life cycle. In a study conducted by Marketing Management Services International Plc (MMSI) it was found that there were several stages when company failure was most likely (Figure 5.1).

G. A. Moore, in his books *Inside the Tornado* (1995) and *Living on the Fault Line* (2000), introduced the concept of the "chasm". The chasm is a break point in the product life cycle where most high tech companies fail. They are able to introduce their product to the market, but fail to be able to sell or deliver it to the main market. Moore describes it as the stage that exists when "the early market's interest wanes but the main stream market is still not

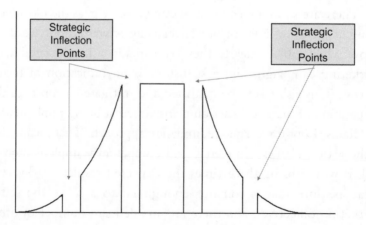

Figure 5.1 Company failure point along the market life cycle

comfortable with the immaturity of the solutions available". Or, put another way, it is at a strategic inflection point where the company's market entry strategy needed to be changed to address the concerns of the main market. The MMSI study, based on data from 22 different countries, found that there was in fact not just one "chasm" but four, and that these coincided with times when a change in business and marketing strategy was required.

As the market matures, a company has to change its strategy; as the market enters decline, a company has to change its strategy; and as the market dies, a company has to change its strategy. The Boston matrix even outlines the strategic changes necessary to be successful in each stage of the product/market life cycle. Yet these chasms are full of the bones of companies not just from the UK but from all around the world. Why do these companies fail and how can we prevent it happening to our company?

How can we quantify the risks?

The first point to note is that many companies do not recognise the stage they have reached in the market/product life cycle. If you don't know where you are, then you almost certainly will not have taken the necessary steps to direct the company from its existing strategy to a winning strategy for the next phase of the life cycle.

Paradigm shift can also move the market, and if the company has not been monitoring it then it may be too late for a change of strategy or it might be impossible to change the strategy because of the investment in the old paradigm. For example, Compaq computers rose to success by seeing the paradigm shifting potential of the 3.5-inch disc drive and overtook IBM, the then market leader, only to fall victim to Dell and its new distribution paradigm. It is not that Compaq did not know what Dell was doing, but Compaq found itself locked into the old channel model and could not respond. In the end HP bought Compaq. The mighty Compaq could have responded to the threat if it had recognised it early enough and accepted its business model's inevitable demise. If it had it would have set up a Dell look-a-like based on the same low-cost distribution model that Dell had developed. This new company would have competed directly with Dell, and while taking some business from Compaq it would have taken business from the others too and prevented Dell from becoming strong enough to challenge Compaq's market leading position. This would have provided a lifeline for Compaq.

There is no market position or risk for which there is no profitable solution, but it involves first recognising the position and then finding the solution quickly enough and being brave enough to implement it.

The most significant indication of things going wrong is when actions that have led to success in the past are no longer effective. I will describe the normal reaction of a company in this real-life example: I was asked by the owner manager of a printing company to help them to market their fantastic window graphics. They had without doubt an excellent product; it never faded and was almost indestructible. You could leave it on the floor of a store for 11 months, simply wash it, and reapply it to your windows where it looked like new. The company had advertised in retail trade magazines for many years and the product sold well. However, there was a problem that the old strategy was failing to deliver the sales required. I investigated the sales figures and was horrified to notice that they were spending more in advertising than they were getting in revenue, and the company was on the brink of bankruptcy. As the sales figures were falling, the management had simply increased their spend on the historically reliable sales strategy of advertising in trade magazines. They had not realised that (a) they had saturated the markets they were selling into, (b) their product was simply too good and (c) they were selling it for too little. The product had reached a strategic inflection point and a change in strategy was required, but the management had not recognised the need until it was virtually too late. This was a classic example of the product focus overriding the marketing focus and the consequences were inevitable.

In another case, I was asked to look at a restaurant chain's performance. The owners were concerned that sales had been falling in the last year or two. I looked over the accounts and after deducting inflation the sales figures showed the classic bell curve shape; it was clear that they had been in decline for many years if inflation was removed from the figures. They needed to urgently review the strategy and make drastic changes if they were going to have any business left. Three things were evident:

(1) The company's failure to recognise the position they were in.
(2) The almost automatic reaction of spending more money on the existing marketing tactics.
(3) Not thinking that the strategy may now be inappropriate for the market conditions.

Had they had effective marketing monitoring tools in place they would have realised that something was going wrong. This would have left them with only two areas where things could be going wrong: the effectiveness of the marketing activity, or the effectiveness of the marketing strategy. Using the STORM (Strategic Tactical Operation Review Management) model (described in Chapter 7), it would have been clear that it was a strategic issue and hence required more than an increase in marketing expenditure or a refocusing of marketing tactics.

It is imperative to good governance that the current market position in which the company operated should be known, and the effectiveness of the marketing function should be monitored. Only by doing this can marketing risk be quantified and the appropriate risk mitigation steps be taken.

A lot of the corporate governance emphasis has spun out of the Enron and WorldCom scandals. At the time of the scandal I wrote an article for the press on how, with the marketing director's input, this type of behaviour could be avoided and shortly after 11 September 2001. I wrote an article on how many companies were using the aftermath of the tragedy to cover up past improprieties and beat the auditor's radar scan.

Here is the edited and abridged version of that article:

As the discredited Labour Party spin-doctor said at the time of the September 11 attacks "it's a good time to bury bad news". Well, as upsetting as it was to hear, this was perfectly true.

The aftermath has allowed a number of companies to bury any skeletons. Turnover falling was expected by the market, which had already reacted and was awaiting it. You were not going to get fired if you wrote off stock or R&D investment or reported a fall in sales, or did not make a quarter's numbers. An opportune time to wipe the slate clean. Where there were any "misclassifications" of expenses, they could have buried within reason in write-offs.

It is for this reason I suspect there will not be too many more Enrons, WordComs and the like, but those that do follow in their wake are going to be huge, having been unable to clear all the skeletons out even with the catastrophic impact of the terrorist action to hide behind.

You must remember that not all companies fit the profile for these type of activities to occur, nor are they in the right types of market, subjected to the right type of market pressure nor have the right management structure to make this kind of fraud likely or undetectable. There are therefore only a limited number of companies that have the capability to be involved in these frauds and of those even fewer have the intent. In addition, new governance requirements and guidelines are restricting the opportunity.

You need both the capability, opportunity and the intent for this type of fraud to be perpetrated and therefore the markets can relax a bit and get back to normal with the caveat that only a few companies are still to fall from grace.

In my book, *Riding the Storm,* I give several examples of "profit flexibility" discovered by our Global Marketing Advantage System (GMAS).

In the course of installing GMAS, a system aimed at strategic and tactical planning alignment and designed to provide marketing advantage, we have found that it has the unfortunate side effect of being able to identify irregularities between the "real world" and the financial records.

In one global company this got us fired, the vice president who hired us transferred from the US to Europe and assigned to "special projects", and her former department, with some 14 staff closed down.

GMAS has uncovered other things including:

- Companies with sales figures that just after the reporting quarter start with a negative number.
- Goods being delivered that had never been ordered.
- Goods being sold by one subsidiary being returned to another company in the group.
- Goods being traded around groups of companies with different accountancy disclosure rules in the different countries making it possible to verify if a sale was genuine or not.
- CAP schemes where promises to buy product at a future date are logged as sales. (Oracle got into a lot of trouble over this one.)
- Bias research designed to verify false market share claims.
- A lot more all invisible to even the most thorough auditors.

Why does the traditional audit not pick up these tricks? Let me give you an example.

We identified in a US multinational what appeared to be a major quality problem: large numbers of goods were being returned as DOA (dead on arrival, that is they did not work when the customer plugged them in). We had no indication of this from the customer satisfaction studies that we conducted on a continuous basis, yet there were complaints about getting goods that had not been ordered and the inconvenience this caused.

The GMAS highlighted issues and recommended we investigate. On investigation we found warehouses full of returned goods awaiting fault testing – more than $30 m worth in one warehouse alone. The fault diagnostic team consisted of only four staff and it would take them several man-years to get around to testing the equipment that was being returned, as this was not their main priority.

We decided to send the next batch of returns to a contractor to have them tested, as it looked on the face of it as if we had a major quality problem that somehow was not impacting on customers. You can imagine our surprise when we read the reports on the tests, "No fault found in any of the units tested".

We immediately dispatched field interviewers to more than 20 countries where these units had been returned from only to discover the goods had been returned not because of a fault but because they had not been ordered. Why had the DOA system been used? They told us that the sales staff told them to use the DOA forms, as this was the fastest way to clear up the problem. We immediately estimated the cost of this and the scale and, rather proud of ourselves, marched off to visit the CEO with the result I described above. We got fired! Not quite what I had expected.

The CEO of this company was, within months, forced out of office but the internal replacement simply covered up the operation and I am sure, like so many other companies with skeletons in their cupboards, used the events of September 11 to readjust their sales figures and write off things, thus burying the past.

How had the audits not detected anything? Well, for one thing the activity involved many different countries. The auditors don't look at sales patterns. They don't ask questions like why all the sales are made on the last week of the last month of the quarter. They don't physically walk around the warehouses, talk to the customers, understand the nature of the business, and don't get much time or support to do their work. Let's face it, even the most upstanding companies begrudge paying auditors' fees, they are expensive and simply tell you what you already know, if you have a good accountancy function and are honest. If on the other hand you are deceitful, clearly some auditors can't detect it. Or if they can they can't do anything other than not sign off the accounts. Which over the last decade has not led to any changes in the European Union's Accounts for example.

It is time for "reality checks" such as those provided by comparing marketing data with the firm's accountancy records.

The need for marketing systems to be capable of verifying accountancy information and to play a key role in corporate governance, especially in the areas of risk quantification, and reporting is now an imperative.

SUMMARY

- Corporate governance and compliance with the various codes of conduct are becoming important to investor groups and hence should be important to companies requiring their support.
- Risk has to be quantified and mitigation formulated, and the marketing function is ideally placed to do both.

CHAPTER 6

INNOVATION AND BUSINESS PLANNING RESEARCH

Without a plan for completion, it just won't happen.

Robert Half

CHICKEN OR EGG?

Marketing plays a vital role in business planning. But does it come first, or does business planning come first? It is rather like asking which came first, the chicken or the egg? As this book is aimed at the marketing director you may guess that I will argue for marketing coming first. Well I do and I don't. It is clear that you have to understand your market and therefore marketing research must come first in all cases apart from in the leading arts-based business and other paradigm-shifting business ideas.

The exception in arts-based businesses and in paradigm shift is the fact that the market does not know the benefits the new paradigm will bring, and being locked into the older paradigm tends only to reflect the marginal or incremental innovations from which the current paradigm could benefit.

In the case of the motor car, research would identify seating, trunk/boot space, greener engines, etc., while the next paradigm shift in transportation may see motor cars relegated to museums and roads dug up for their rubble content. Market research would not help to define the new transport paradigm unless you detach the individuals from the existing paradigm. This can be done but often provides a *Star Trek* "Beam me up Scotty" answer to transport, which may not be a realistic possibility with current science.

There are techniques in research, such as conjoint analysis, that can help us to identify value behind products, and such techniques can be used to help to define the likely attributes of paradigm shift. The reality is that it may be something you have to invent, design, draw, and build before you can assess its market potential, and even then you need a powerful individual who can translate his vision of what the future product will be to have any chance of success. It is unlikely that early versions will achieve the full potential of the inventor's vision.

The three sources of traditional business market research are based around (a) improving or identifying a unique selling proposition in existing or developing markets, (b) making incremental improvement; or (c) accepting what the science will allow.

The artist marketing innovation model is simply to believe in the art form and create the object, then to communicate with the prospective audience and win acceptance, usually to the disdain of the art establishment of the time. It is very unlikely that a market research focus group would have identified a market for Picasso's work. He had to create, then seek acceptance, and introduce a change in the mind set of what constituted art. This is why many artists live a very poor life and why very few succeed. However, almost all the great artists have changed the perception of "What is art?".

In developing paradigm-shifting technology or ideas do not expect to be welcomed by the existing establishment. Many conspiracy theorists have speculated about the number of inventions that either the car industry or the oil industry may have suppressed to preserve the automobile and oil-based transport system.

UNIQUE SELLING PROPOSITION

A unique selling proposition (USP) can be easily established from traditional marketing research, ranging from focus groups and other qualitative research methods to quantitative research to determine the extent of the potential market.

In financial services the USP has been used to identify categories of motorist that have better risk profiles than others. Compliance and reporting requirements in the banking community have also had the by-product of allowing the profiling of customers and the identification of segments and life stages where there are obvious product gaps and a new market opportunity.

Monitoring of customer complaints about competitive products can generate USP. Having your call centre in the UK has recently become important to some buyers of services who are angered by the poor language skills of some overseas call centre operators.

It should be noted that a USP need not be a single feature translated into an individual benefit; it can be a combination of features that generate unique benefits to any particular market or segment.

INCREMENTAL IMPROVEMENTS

This is by far the most widely spread area of competitive advantage, making the existing product better, faster and cheaper – for example, the development of the humble duster into a host of dust-busting innovations ranging from disposable anti-static dusters to specialist window blind products. The customer and brainstorming are valuable sources of ideas, as are techniques such as *Mad Cards Innovation* for use with groups of internal staff or customers.

Mad Cards innovation

(*Formula for innovation and market advantage*)

"Mad Cards" incorporate the latest thinking on innovation and creativity and go far beyond brainstorming. This programmed approach to innovation can revolutionise your creativity and develop and generate incremental innovations that will keep your products and services ahead of the competition. It can generate revolutionary new product ideas and concepts.

Based in the real world but with a pedigree in top quality research, "Mad Cards" will take you step by step through a process that is guaranteed to make even the most reluctant innovator innovative.

The techniques are of use in a multitude of businesses where incremental improvement will bring a marketing advantage for your particular product or service, be it biotechnology or garden-ware.

Mad Cards basics

Apply the following formula and stand back as the ideas fly.

M – Multiplication
A – Addition
D – Division

C – Connection
A – Attribute dependency
R – Replacement
D – Displacement
S – Substitution

M – Multiplication

Multiply the features of the product or service and list the new benefits.

Let's take, for example, your laptop. What would happen if you multiplied the components and had, say, two keyboards or monitors or multiple processors? Multiple screens would enable people around the table to see your screen; multiple keyboards could mean easier collaboration on a document being worked on in a meeting; multiple processors could mean ultra fast processing of graphics.

A – Addition

Add new benefits to the product, then describe the features that would deliver that benefit.

For example, essential information could be retained on screen when a PDA battery ran out. This would allow advertising or emergency checklists to be displayed on an aircraft monitor even when the power has failed.

D – Division

Split the components of the product's attributes and explore the benefits.

Look at the major components and skills used by a boat builder and determine where they could otherwise be applied. For example, fibreglass building expertise, installation of kitchens and bathrooms in confined spaces, waterproofing, installation of communications and GPS equipment. From these components explore other applications of the skills expertise.

C – Connection

Explore the way the product or service is linked to its environment (space, time, location, etc.). How could it be linked better or be more useful or timely?

On-line shopping is dependent on Internet connectivity in the home or office. What if it could be accessed in store. You could place an on-line repeat order of items purchased at that visit for next week or for daily delivery.

A – Attribute dependency

Changing the key component variables.

Scottish porridge is traditionally eaten when it is hot and soft. What could we do with it when it is cold and firm?

R – Replacement

Substitute part of the product for something else in the immediate environment.

Replace an office flat-bed document scanner by a photocopier scanner, creating an all-in-one system that scans, photocopies and prints.

D – Displacement

Removing one of the intrinsic features of the product and service.

Removing the office from a services office business would result in an answering service, virtual address, mail-handling and meeting room hire business.

S – Substitution

Substitute one of the major components for something from another environment.

For example, replacing the wheels on a motorbike with skis.

All of these techniques in the Mad Cards armoury generate lots of ideas. Some of these ideas will not survive scrutiny, but others may not just survive scrutiny but become a market differentiator and give the investing company an incremental lead over competitors. I challenge you to try mad cards on your leading product and service. I think you will be surprised by what you come up with.

TRADITIONAL MARKET RESEARCH

Whether you use mad cards or brainstorming or any other technique for developing your business concept, you need to determine if there is a market for your idea. This will involve market research.

You will not have reached the position of marketing director without having a thorough understanding of marketing research techniques, ranging from secondary research to primary research. Therefore, I do not propose to explain the techniques here, but only wish to mention some of the latest techniques that can aid you in undertaking effective, efficient market research.

You will recall from the breakthrough marketing model described earlier, that the objective of any research is to do as little as possible, but not less than is required; that is to say, gather "only needed information". Therefore, knowing what you need to know, now and in the short-term, and building research pools, are all vital to any efficient research you undertake.

The fundamental issue is to determine what you "need to know", and clearly separate that from what you "would like to know" and what "would be interesting to know". When you are involved in business planning your research is wider than simply the market. There are other directors who wish to ask questions and have their own information requirements. Their issues should also be addressed if the business plan is to be solid enough to support a successful business. You may have to educate them into only asking for information they really need, and if possible you should coordinate all the various information requirements into a single survey, thereby keeping as many environmental variables as constant as possible in the research time window.

Irrefutable research

If we are going to gather only "needed research" then the quality of what is gathered must be irrefutable. The shorter time frame needed to gather this research also means that there is more time for analysis and interpretation, or turning the data into competitive market intelligence. With such a reliance on research it is imperative that we use the very best agencies with, at the very minimum, BS 7911 or its new international standard ISO 20252; also, the firm used should be Investors in People and BS EN ISO 9001 registered for marketing research and consultancy services. In this way we can expect reliable information to be generated – although reliability is not enough, it must also be valid.

Let me take you through the research questions that you need to answer to have a chance of getting reliable, valid, irrefutable research data that can be translated into real intelligence and, therefore, competitive advantage.

As I have already mentioned, the breakthrough marketing model limits the amount of research that we should conduct to "needed information only".

In any business plan you will be able to identify critical assumptions upon which the plan is based, and these must be verified and clearly fit within the "needed information" because if they prove to be erroneous the whole business plan can flounder.

Research initially gathered in the strategic planning process, can also be required in the implementation plans derived from the strategy. For example:

- The business plan gives rise to, among others, the financial, marketing, personnel, quality and facilities plans, and their derivatives.
- The marketing plan in turn gives rise to the product, pricing, promotion and distribution plans, and their derivatives.
- The promotional plan gives rise to the media, public relations, sales promotion, sales plans, and their derivatives.
- The sales promotion plan gives rise to the exhibition, point of sales materials, and their derivatives.
- These plans give rise to individuals' KPIs and their actions.

All these steps require some research or at least access to the corporate knowledge base. When considering needed information, a thorough understanding of what information is essential at each stage of the cascade, down to the individual's KPIs, has to be considered in order to maximise the benefits from each piece of research data gathered.

If we are going to be efficient and gather only needed information, then we should endeavour not to reinvent the wheel too often or gather the same information twice.

The need for a corporate knowledge base is therefore obvious. It will reduce the learning time for new staff and generate research required throughout the organisation. If we gather the information in one exercise, in the full knowledge of who will be interested in using it – or at least in keeping track of the sources – we can conduct the research to provide only the needed information quickly, effectively and efficiently.

When specifying what is "needed information" it is necessary to consider all the potential users within the organisation. It is also necessary to have a storage system and, more importantly, a retrieval system in place to access the information collected. You should keep accurate records of sources of information and, when gathering information from respondents, to keep in mind that you will most probably need to talk to them again. Perhaps the most important step is to record where DIKI (Data, Information, Knowledge and Intelligence) is used in plans.

In the real world, planning has to be performed in a real-time/right-time mode as needed changes to strategy cannot wait, perhaps up to, 12 months until the next planning cycle. If you need to make changes because of new DIKI then you need to know where the old DIKI was used and hence which parts of the plan will be affected by the new DIKI. Let me give you an example: If we assumed, in the original business plan, that over the next year interest rates would remain within 0.5% of the then current base rate and that this is critical to our investment strategy, then if we find that the interest rates are now likely to exceed that figure we need to review the parts of our business plan that are reliant upon that assumption. However, it will not be only the original business plan that will be affected but all the department plans that have been composed to achieve the business objectives. Which plans now need to be reviewed and which do not? Unless you have tracked where that information has been used, you will not know, and the result may be that some impacted plans will not be amended while others that were not impacted will be subjected to a review and result in a complete waste of resources.

Before gathering any information you must answer the questions below to be sure it is needed.

Why do we need this information?

The DIKI gathered must be critical, or at least important to your organisation. If data collected is simply "nice to know" or routine, then it should not be gathered. Therefore every research request or study should have its purpose clearly recorded and attached to all the various iterations of the findings.

I am often surprised by the number of research commissions in which we are asked to gather information that will never be used or is already known by the company. Another source of wasted resources is the standing survey that is no longer relevant but is conducted none the less because of habit. All research needs to justify its existence. Whenever you see a report, ask yourself: What is the importance and relevance of the information being presented? If you can't use the information or turn it into knowledge or market intelligence, then something is wrong and you should be questioning why this information is being gathered, or at least being given to you to read.

What will you do with the results?

There must be a use for the information being gathered. When reviewing questions on a questionnaire, I often come across double questions such as "How happy were you with the new product and service provided?" The respondent is normally asked to answer the question on some form of a satisfaction scale. What does the answer mean and what will you do with the answers given? If a respondent is dissatisfied, where is the problem? Is the dissatisfaction with the product or the service provided? Who should we report this information to: service or product development or both? If the respondent was actually unhappy with the service but loved the product, how would we know? Will taking action on the strength of the results leave a department searching for a fault that does not exist? To avoid this type of problem, ensure that the questions asked will provide the answers needed to be actionable, and therefore it is important to know what the results will be used for. In the marketing context this may not present you with any problems, but when you are gathering DIKI for other functions its use may not be at first obvious. This particular question would not be used or recommended by a professional marketing research organisation and is known as a double stem error.

Always consider how the research will be used. Mock up the answers and ask the recipients of the findings: Are these results going to provide the information you need to take action? Only commission research that will generate "actionable" data: that is, provide you with enough data or information that you can act on the results you get.

What would we do if we did not have the data?

Can you get by without the research results or would you be taking an unnecessary or even unacceptable risk to do so?

Some organisations give customer satisfaction research only lip service, despite it now being part of the ISO 9001 requirements. If you do not conduct customer satisfaction research, then in the short term nothing much changes, and if you are very close to a small number of customers you will probably consider this research as not needed information because the customers' views are already known and reinforced daily. You would be right in this circumstance, but if you have multiple customers served by third parties, then customer satisfaction research is vital to numerous parts of the organisation.

The chances are that a variety of departments within the organisation are all trying to survey the same customers and causing more harm than good. By considering how the results will be used within the context of the whole organisation, needed information can be gathered efficiently without risking survey fatigue in your customer base.

Who needs the information?

Listing all the staff that can benefit from this information is a first step in building the ENT (Enterprise Neuron Trail) that I mentioned earlier. Sticking with the customer satisfaction example, who would benefit in your organisation from measuring customer satisfaction? I think you would be pushed to find someone who would not – especially if we consider the internal customers who receive internally provided support and services.

In Cisco Systems, staff bonuses use a multiplier on individuals' and departments' internal or external customer satisfaction scores. If facilities don't provide you with good service, you let them know that it will affect their bonuses if they don't improve. Everyone needs customer satisfaction scores, but the perspective on the results is different throughout the organisation. What service wants to know in customer satisfaction terms is quite different from what new product development wants to know. It is important to get a thorough view on what each perspective is going to be before commissioning customer satisfaction research.

Do we already have the information?

This may sound simplistic and obvious, but before commencing research make sure that the information is not already being gathered within the company. I have previously been commissioned to do research only to find that, as I start to talk to the staff, the same or very similar information has already been gathered. On one occasion I was handed a report that had been completed by a student on placement and contained almost all the information the client required.

In one company for whom I worked, I estimated that they were spending $3 million a year on various research exercises and talking to their customers, most of which was a duplication of effort. I recommended that, as a first step, they find out who is commissioning research and that all research should be cleared through a Central Research Agency in one area of their business prior to commencement. By implementing this, research bills were cut from an estimated $3 million to $900,000! Seven different parts of the business were surveying the same customer group, asking almost the same questions, each one unaware of the others' activities. Each group charged the research to a different budget code making it impossible for the finance department to clearly identify true corporate research expenditure.

Have we diagnosed the knowledge requirement accurately?

I have been talking about customer satisfaction research, but why do we really want it? The obvious answer is because we want satisfied customers. However, if we apply the "why test", first developed by children just after they learn to talk, we come across a different reason.

> *Parent* Go to bed.
> *Child* Why?
> *Parent* Because you need your sleep.
> *Child* Why?
> *Parent* Your body needs time to get refreshed for tomorrow.
> *Child* Why?
> *Parent* Go to bed NOW!

Just as it can be infuriating to parents, it is extremely powerful at getting to the root of the issue. Perhaps because of our early experiences of using the word, we forget to ask it often enough when we became adults.

Question Why do we want to know about customer satisfaction?

Answer So we can provide better products and services.

Question Why?

Answer Because we want loyal customers.

Question Why?

Answer Because loyal customers will stay with us longer and make us more profit.

From the "why" test, it is clear that it is not customer satisfaction in itself that is important, but how this impacts on customer loyalty and how that leads to increased profits. There is an old saying that you have loyal customers right up to the time they buy from your competitor. This shows that while loyalty is important, what causes it to break down is more important. Chasing customer satisfaction without understanding its "elasticity" is just getting a part of the needed information. Customer satisfaction must be viewed in the context of loyalty, competitors, cost to improve, and break factors. (What causes the loyalty to break down and at what point does it occur?)

If we look at a branded computer and compare it to a non-branded one, an owner of the branded computer will, when choosing his next computer, be influenced not only by the experience with the current computer, but also by many other factors. When other factors draw the brand-buying customer to buy the generic product, just how strong these factors have to be is known as the degree of "loyalty elasticity". At some point the factors will exceed the loyalty elasticity and loyalty will break down. Therefore, simply measuring customer satisfaction is not always enough. Loyalty and loyalty limits have also to be understood for customer satisfaction data to be actionable, and for that action to effectively strengthen customer loyalty and improve its elasticity.

While on the subject of customer loyalty, research with numerous clients allowed the development of a loyalty model. Many factors have been found to impact loyalty, and some of them are listed here:

- Problem/need: There must be a need and that need must be recognised.
- Changing need: Needs never stay static, they change over time.
- Search for solution: Your solution must be seen to be found.
- Purchase channel: There must be a means of purchasing your service or product.
- Authority: The person with the need has to have the authority to purchase your solution.
- Relationship strength: Both personal and business relationships are important.
- Actual value delivered.
- Perceived value of the product or service.
- Involvement: If the buyer has been instrumental in designing the solution, he will be more inclined to be loyal.
- Recommendation: The more the better.
- RoI (Return on Investment): This must be based on three factors: how certain, how soon, and how much.
- Competitor attention.
- Susceptibility of buyer to bribery, blackmail or other corruption.
- Your firm's performance against experience with other vendors generally.
- Inertia.
- Problems unresolved or taken out of proportion.
- New staff and knowledge acquisition by client may remove need for external supplier.
- Familiarisation.

- Customer satisfaction and its communication within the client organisation.
- Budget changes.
- Responsibility movements.
- Staff turnover, promotion or new staff appointments.

Perhaps you can add to this list, but, in summary, RS (relationship strength), CN (continued need), CS (customer satisfaction) and PV (perceived value) bind a customer to your service or product. If you fail to monitor these, you will surely lose the customer.

In what format must the information be presented to be most usable?

Gathering information in a non-usable form is a waste of time. I have heard of marketing departments commissioning benchmarking information with a view to publicising their ranking only to find that the information they have gathered has restrictions on its distribution, and its use for marketing purposes is expressly forbidden.

The classic examples are what I call the "single number reports". These reports produce a single number, say, for customer satisfaction, and you are expected to do something if the customer satisfaction falls and you are presumed to have done something right if it rises. Unfortunately, many managers do not truly understand statistics and those that do agree with the British Victorian Prime Minister Benjamin Disraeli when he said, "there are lies, dammed lies and statistics". What is happening when the customer satisfaction score rises or falls depends on a number of factors, as well as the actual level of customer satisfaction. There are margins of error in all research and when you see a single figure, you can be sure that it is wrong. There is always a margin of error to take into account. You will have observed that pollsters report their results as, for example, 78% plus or minus 2%. What they are saying is that the real number is somewhere between 76% and 80%. If the next result was 76% plus or minus 2% would there be a difference? Well, there may be, but that is not certain. Returning to the customer satisfaction example, one week's results showing customer satisfaction at 78% and the next week's showing it at 76% may mean that nothing has changed. In order for the information to be useful, the needed information is not the customer satisfaction score alone, but the score plus the margin of error.

How reliable and valid must the information be?

Above I mentioned the margin of error. If you need to know something accurately, this must be specified and be within the realms of reality. At board level it may be acceptable to review accounts to the nearest million, at department level to the nearest thousand, while individual projects may be to the nearest dollar, pound, euro or yen. All of these figures, one assumes, are reliable. The margins of errors may then be in proportion to the scale being used. A margin of error equivalent to rounding to the nearest million may be acceptable at board level, but no error is accepted in a petty cash report.

There are two important concepts in any type of survey: reliability and validity.

* *Reliability*: Reliability is the consistency of the survey tool. If I conduct a survey by telephone month on month, I can produce reliable data just as I can if I survey on the web month on month. However, if I survey by e-mail one month and by telephone the next, then even although each method may be reliable I will have created an unreliable methodology. In other words, the results would not be consistent month on month,

because web-based surveys tend to have negative shift values compared to telephone research.

- *Validity*: A valid survey tool is accurate in serving the purpose for which it is designed and provides correct information. The fact that a telephone customer satisfaction survey generated higher satisfaction scores than a web-based survey, suggests that either method, or indeed both, may not be valid. However, they both become valid if the purpose is to monitor a trend, because both reflect the actual customer satisfaction reliably. Figure 6.1 shows that when the same populations of customer satisfaction are monitored by both telephone research and e-mail, they invite a web-based survey (I have removed the margins of error for clarity).

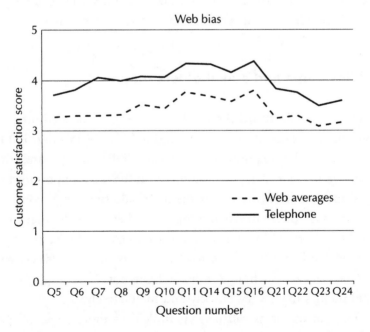

Figure 6.1   Customer satisfaction variance by method adopted

VALIDITY AND RELIABILITY

An interesting statement could be made at this point: if a survey is unreliable, then it is invalid. Valid instruments are always reliable, but reliable tools are not always valid. Testing my previous example, telephone and web-based research are both reliable, that is, they produce consistent results. However, they don't produce the same answers, therefore one or both may not be valid. They both follow a very similar pattern and would appear to be correlated to each other, and to the actual customer satisfaction. If the purpose is to map the trends in customer satisfaction, then, taken individually, we find that they clearly do that. This suggests that they are valid instruments to monitor trends, if not the absolute customer satisfaction score. Therefore, as they are valid, they should also be reliable, which they are.

If you see unreliable surveys, be quite clear that the information they are providing is invalid. Like accounts, they can only be valid if they have been recorded in a consistent manner.

Publics maps and stakeholders maps

Having taken on board the need to gather only needed information, the next question is: To whom should we be talking? Publics maps chart the organisation's external relationships and their exchange balance. They help to focus on the most important relationships and what influences them. In addition, they consist of several layers of detail. At the top layer they map the main relationships, both influential and transactional, while at the more detailed level they will link to databases or industry directories. Using a package such as Ygnius or Idons for Thinking, you can build publics maps very quickly and interactively.

Each of the arms can be hyperlinked to more pages of maps or to documents or websites. It is very easy using this software to

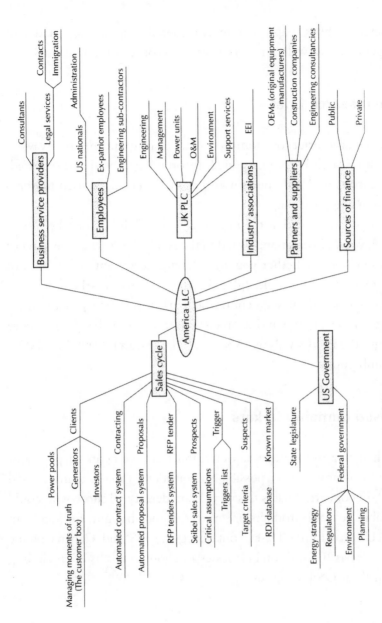

Figure 6.2 Example of first level publics map power industry

generate publics maps. The level of detail required is a matter of judgement and will vary from organisation to organisation.

The research brief

The research brief for monitoring and testing outlines the ways in which research is commissioned, recorded, gathered and reported. The results will only be as useful as the brief that is used to commission the research.

If you request that the rate of growth of the market be monitored, you may be disappointed in the results because the researcher will not know whether you are referring to the rate of growth of the market as a whole (global), the national market, regional market or a specific segment of the market in which you are operating. In short, the more precise your research brief, the more precise the results will be. Above all, the research brief must NOT be ambiguous.

Closed domain markets

With increasing storage capacity and improvements in processor speed it is now almost possible to consider all markets in a closed domain context. That is to say, we can identify all those who could possibly buy our products or services. I once bought, for $35 from CD USA, a four CD set containing the US and Canada phone book. It has 104 million businesses and households listed, including 16 million US businesses.

Quality assurance

Quality assurance in research is paramount, and to get close to irrefutable research results you need to ensure that your research provider at least meets if not exceeds the following quality standards or their equivalents: BS EN ISO 9001, BS 7911, ISO 20252, MRQSA and IIP. MMSI Plc is registered/accredited to all four and these should be considered the starting point for achievement of irrefutable research.

BS EN ISO 9001

BS EN ISO 9001 is the international quality assurance standard. What is covered by the quality standard is specified in the scope. For example, MMSI Plc is quality assured to BS EN ISO 9001 "for the provision of market research and consultancy services". It is wise to check that the scope of registration is appropriate to the type of work you require the partner or contractor to perform.

BS 7911

BS 7911 is the British quality standard for organisations conducting market research and sets the minimum standard for quality control and research design and execution. This standard was established in 1998.

ISO 20252

This is the international standard and is the lowest common denominator between countries. It is slightly less onerous than BS 7911 in some regards and stricter in others.

MRQSA

MRQSA is the quality assurance standard of the UK's Market Research Society and outlines the procedures that must be followed as a minimum to ensure quality in research outputs.

IIP (Investors in People)

The Investors in People standard is a quality standard for staff. It provides a framework that organisations use to help them to improve performance. Organisations that meet the standard have to show that they are committed to developing their people; that they have clear goals; that their investment in people directly helps them to meet these goals; and that they understand the impact that this investment has on staff performance. I believe that, at the end of the day, it is the quality of the research staff that makes the difference. A well-trained, motivated staff with a high level of integrity is essential in providing irrefutable research data.

Codes of conduct

As well as quality assurance there are codes of conduct for most of the professions that conduct research. In the UK, compliance with the code of conduct of the Market Research Society and/or the Chartered Institute of Marketing, and/or the Management Consultants Association, is what you should insist upon from consultants and research providers. It goes without saying that these codes must be strictly adhered to by the members of chartered and other professional bodies.

ACCESS TO INFORMATION

As important as the conduct of the research, is the access to the research results and analysis. Flooding people with information is counter-productive, while depriving them of it is equally bad. Have you ever been at a meeting where you have been annoyed at not being informed about something, only to be told that it was in such and such a report that you routinely receive?

Customer Satisfaction
Attributes and correlations over time

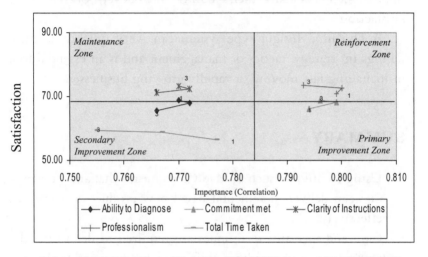

Attribute correlation to Top2 score: 1)Start of reporting [Q2'04], 2) Average Q1'04-Q1'05, 3) Q2'05.

Figure 6.3   Dynamic Insight reporting tool

The ability to sift down through the intelligence to the raw data offers considerable advantages over other reporting and balanced scorecard tools, and this, coupled with real-time/right-time data, allows managers to see situations developing long before they become an issue that will be reflected in higher level monitors. For example: A call centre manager can view the customer satisfaction results coming in while the call centre is running. Indications of problems reflected in the customer satisfaction scores can be related to a specific product line, or even operator, and corrected before they become bad enough to affect the overall customer satisfaction scores that are reported to a more senior level. If the manager fails to address the issue, then the senior level staff will be alerted to a problem that needs their attention. A typical result of this type of system is an overall improvement in customer satisfaction scores of around an incredible 30%, and this improvement is sustained. Introducing a six sigma or other continuous improvement system then builds the level of customer satisfaction.

A Dynamic Insight type system can, very quickly, identify failings in strategy, tactics or management and is an essential tool in managing fast-moving or rapidly growing businesses.

SUMMARY

- Using techniques such as Mad Cards means that almost everyone can deliver incremental-based new product development effectively.
- Care and specialist techniques are required to determine the true potential of paradigm-shifting technology and traditional research can provide misleading results.
- Getting market intelligence to the right person who can use it profitably is a major challenge.

CHAPTER 7

BUSINESS PLANNING PROCESS

There is only one thing in business that is certain and that's change. I don't know what tomorrow is going to be like, but I do know this – it's bound to be different from yesterday and today.

Henry Ford

In the previous chapter we explored the importance of research in the business planning process, but what is the process that should be followed in business planning at boardroom level?

The process begins by the board confirming, modifying or developing the corporate vision, mission and values. From these are prepared the SMART (Specific, Measurable, Achievable, Realistic and Time-framed) objectives. The individual directors take on the task of converting the overall objectives into specific objectives for their areas of responsibility. They then verify that the objectives are in fact achievable, realistic and can be accomplished in the time frame stipulated. The feedback from this exercise results in the development of the corporate strategy and the building of integrated plans to achieve the objectives within the vision, mission and values of the enterprise.

To recap: The board of directors collectively:

• develop a corporate vision;
• from the vision they develop the mission and frame this within the corporate values;
• set the first draft SMART objectives.

The individual board members then research these objectives and determine what they need to achieve; the objectives within the time frame; or prepare an explanation for the board on why the objective, as set, cannot be achieved.

The board then reconvene and confirm or adjust the objectives – a process known as "defining the achievable".

The board then formulate the strategy and the individual board members construct their departmental and other implementation plans.

The board meet again to finalise the plans and ensure integration between the various departments, in the process drawing out the critical assumptions and determining which require monitoring and which will require to be researched.

The board then sign off the plans, all discussion stops, and the focus is switched to achieving the objectives set. The board then take on a monitoring, command and control role.

The critical assumptions (CAs) are monitored, as is implementation, and the strategy is reviewed if a CA is compromised or the review date is reached.

Let's now look at each of these stages in a little more detail.

CORPORATE VISION MISSION AND VALUES

Vision

The corporate vision is the capturing of the aspirations of the board of directors for the business.

The vision tends to be larger than merely generating profits and encapsulates a more noble purpose that can inspire others to strive for. It can, and often is, captured in the company's slogan, which is aimed at summing up the essence of the organisation in a memorable and evocative way.

The slogan must capture the basic promise of the company and thus be the embodiment of the company's vision.

"The best a man can get"	Gillette
"We try harder"	Avis
"Helping your business grow"	MMSI
"Every little helps"	Tesco
"See what you can do"	O₂
"The power of dreams"	Honda
"I'm loving it"	McDonald's
"The world's local bank"	HSBC
"We make the net work"	Sun Microsystems
"Beyond Petroleum"	BP
"Bringing the best to everyone we touch"	Estee Lauder Company

The corporate slogan should not be confused with a catch line used in a specific promotion. Although the two terms are often used interchangeably, the corporate slogan sums up the company's vision, not just a specific brand promise.

Having articulated the vision and, if possible, encapsulated that vision in a memorable corporate slogan, where we are going has been established. What follows is the mission.

Mission

The mission is the statement of why the business exists. It addresses the question: Why should customers, investors and employees choose this company. It must encapsulate its publics/stakeholders benefits and may include reference to the environment and being a good citizen.

Time should be taken to carefully craft the mission statement as it should act as a guiding light for the company and ensure that the key stakeholders can understand their value in their relationship with the company.

Ideally the mission statement should be short, flexible and unique to your organisation. "Unique" is the most difficult of these to achieve and you will have already read many mission statements that could easily be used to describe a number of companies. The statement has to be flexible so that it does not straitjacket the company, but not so loose that there is no focus.

A common failure is the mission that reads: "we want to be number one". When studying the Strategic Marketing of Educational Institutions I was amazed to find how many educational institutions aimed for the number one slot, which, naturally enough, only one of them could eventually fill. Clearly there were going to be a lot of disappointed colleges. That said, many US firms manage to define their position as number one so uniquely that only they will be able to fill that position – for example, to be the number one, in terms of sales volume and value, provider of camera equipment to the professional photographer market in Birmingham, Alabama, etc.

One of my favourite mission statements is still that of the Scout movement:

To promote the development of young people in achieving their full physical, intellectual, social, and spiritual potentials, as individuals, as responsible citizens and as members of their local, national and international communities.

You will know when you have chosen the correct mission statement when it appeals to nobler goals than the mere pursuit of profit.

In the consultancy market it has always been necessary to attract the best talent, and this is traditionally done in the USA by targeting the Ivy League colleges. Two great rivals, McKinsey & Co. Inc. and Coopers & Lybrand were pitching to attract the best graduates. Compare their mission statements and answer the question: Which would you rather work for?

A: *Our mission is to be the leading business adviser.*

B: *To help our clients make a positive, lasting and substantial improvement in their performance and to build a great firm that is able to attract, develop, excite, and retain exceptional people.*

Well, if like me you feel you are exceptional, then there is only one choice: McKinsey & Co. mission statement B. The mission statement is a marketing tool and therefore should not be left solely to non-marketing minded board members to construct.

Values

I feel that the values statement has become necessary because the mission statement was becoming too large as it attempts to address too many issues for a single statement. The values statement enables a lot of the candyfloss to be removed from the mission statement and can be more meaningfully and specifically stated. The values state unambiguously the moral code and ethical standards under which the company does business. It includes its stance on compliance with the law, ethical investment policy, and environmental and standards. It should be unambiguous and state clearly what is expected from your employees and what customers can expect when dealing with your organisation.

Objectives

The objectives of the company should be SMART – that is, Specific, Measurable, Achievable, Realistic and Time-framed. In this way they can be measured and success or failure judged openly.

The objectives must be considered as a whole and not just as individual statements to avoid conflict between them. Considerable effort should be spent on ensuring compatibility between objectives because, as the old adage goes, "What gets measured gets done".

Not obvious, but essential to record, is the critical assumptions that have been relied upon to develop the objectives. If, during the course of time, critical assumptions become compromised, then it is important that the objectives are revisited immediately to determine if they are still realistic and achievable within the time frame. If they are not, then immediate strategic changes may be necessary.

Strategy

Having set the objectives it is necessary to formulate the strategy that will ensure that they are achieved within the specified time frame. The strategy is the route map and details the courses of action that will be necessary to achieve the objective. The strategy is the blueprint of the objective, containing the necessary foundation work that needs to be undertaken, and contains details of all the activities and associated plans that must come together in order for the objectives to be achieved.

Plans

The various departments need to design all the components for the blueprint and detail exactly what actions must be taken, by whom, when to achieve the various steps in the strategy, and the overall objectives.

The linkage between the objectives, strategy and plans should be strong and reinforced regularly. If not, they will disintegrate into plans that are followed regardless of any strategic or objective changes and actions taken that may or may not contribute to achieving the overall objective. It is quite common in sales-led organisations for the marketing strategy to be totally ignored, provided that the sales targets are being met by some other route that may compromise long-term corporate success. For example, selling solutions that do not fit the customers' needs may generate short-term sales growth but will destroy the company's value in the longer term as customers stop buying and move to competitors.

Scenario testing

We are ready for any unforeseen event that may or may not occur – Dan Quayle

A very worthwhile exercise, which should be scheduled after the majority of the planning exercises have been completed, is the testing of the plan against various likely market conditions or scenarios. This can generate responses and courses of action that would be adopted should the market or environmental conditions not be exactly as forecast.

Date stamp and critical assumptions

Throughout the planning process, critical assumptions and the ENT will have been established. This means that what is critical to whom and why will be known or at least suspected. To this has to be added a date stamp for revisiting, rather like the electrical safety notice on electrical cables in offices when it states when next it needs inspecting. There are only two eventualities that will cause you to revisit the plan: (1) the date for review becoming due or (2) the compromise of a critical assumption. Regular annual reviews tend to be very ineffective because such reviews very rarely coincide with major market events such as independent market share statistics or market reports being published, and therefore you can review the plan on Monday to find that a report that was issued on Tuesday makes the work obsolete. It is better to review the plan only when you have some material need to do so and not on some annual date in the calendar.

You could view the date stamp-based reviews as preventative maintenance. A compromised critical assumption is more akin to a breakdown. This breakdown can be severe, or is more likely an indication of imminent failure. It is very rare for a well-prepared strategy to be completely derailed by a single event, but a gradual compromise is more likely. For example, if your investment plans are based on interest rates being below 5% and at the planning stage they were 3%, it would be most unlikely, in a stable economy, that they would exceed 5% in a single interest rate rise; but gradual interest rate rises of 0.5% quarter on quarter or rising inflation figures would be a strong indicator that the investment strategy should be revisited.

HOW LONG SHOULD YOU SPEND ON BUSINESS PLANNING?

Some have argued that you should spend as long as it takes, but not a minute longer, while others set specific time frames. The volume of detail ranges from major work assignments to a simple one-page business plan. The planning process, in many firms, is spread over three months – just prior to the end of the financial year to the start of the new one. If a real-time planning model is adopted and a flexible balanced scorecard system is in place, strategy can be altered when required in a very short period of time, so there is no need to have an annual planning cycle. Planning happens when it is necessary, and standing orders maintain the status quo at all other times.

If you are in a small company or even a medium-sized company, I am happy to recommend the *One Page Business Plan* book written by Jim Horan because, whether or not you realistically can summarise your business plan in just one page, it helps you to focus on the important points that you must communicate in the business planning process, and has a very practical approach to helping you to formulate the business plan.

Combining the techniques of breakthrough marketing and the planning process discussed above, will enable you to contribute successfully to the overall business plan ensuring that the marketing importance of the associated documents, statements and other public documents are aligned with the marketing image the company is seeking to project to its various associates.

The question should perhaps be rephrased as: Once you have established the business plan, how often should it be revisited? My view is that it should not, unless its review date is reached or critical assumptions show indications of becoming compromised. I have developed a model that I have called STORM to help to determine when a company should review its strategy.

STORM

The world is not interested in the storms you encountered, but did you bring in the ship?

William McFee

STORM is an acronym for "Strategic Tactical Operational Review Management" and is illustrated in Figure 7.1, which maps out the

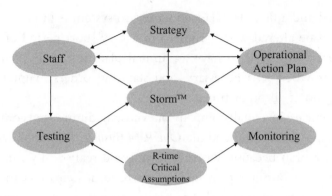

Figure 7.1 STORM model

seven areas that contribute to the STORM theory of managing the strategic planning process.

Strategy

We have defined the strategy above and this is the starting point for the STORM model. The strategy has to be documented and the expected indicators of success clearly defined.

Staff

Staff often detect the conditions that may lead to a critical assumption being compromised, and they form the critical factor in the achievement of any plan.

When objectives are not being met it is important, early on, to determine where the fault lies. The fault will lie in one of three places: in the action plans; in the strategy; or in the staff's implementation of the plans.

When a plan starts to fail, the STORM model helps to determine where the problem lies and can separate poor staff performance from a poor implementation plan, or even a flaw in strategy.

All three are monitored: the staff are monitored through individual scorecards or/and key performance indicators (KPIs); operational plans are monitored by the achievement of milestones; and the strategy is monitored by success of the corporate mission and all the objectives leading up to its achievement.

Operational action plans

The operational action plans guide the staff in the actions they need to take to achieve the objectives via the determined strategy. Operational plans must be aligned with the strategy and not permitted to drift. Action plans are just that: they are tasks which, if performed as prescribed, should achieve the desired outcome within the time allowed. The first indication of things not going as planned is often the failure of some action plan to deliver the desired outcomes on time. The STORM centre monitors the action plans against the expected outcomes and will alert staff to a missed deadline and request an explanation. This may or may not provide adequate reasons, but will trigger a line manager to investigate.

Real-time critical assumptions

The planning process, described above, generates a list of critical assumptions upon which KPIs, action plans, objectives and the strategy have been based. These need to be monitored or tested to prevent them from becoming compromised without the board being aware.

Monitoring

The critical assumptions should, in general terms, be monitored and any indication that they are becoming compromised should be investigated.

Testing

Some critical assumptions are so important that they should not simply be monitored; they must be tested. This may involve conducting continuous research or ad hoc research studies, but in any event they must be tested to turn them from an assumption into a fact, or at least to determine the probability of occurrence and hence the risk that must be accepted or managed.

Real options

In some cases where the risk is quantified and the consequences of the critical assumption being compromised are severe, it makes prudent sense to consider some form of real option mitigation. In the case of an energy supplier, who is exposed to market price fluctuations, it may be necessary for the trading company to have their own generating capacity as a kind of stop loss situation should they be unable to buy energy at the right price to fulfil their contract position. The cost of real options is balanced against the cost of loss without any options. Using scenario planning and quantifying the probability of occurrence allows risk positions to be determined and real options investigated. It also enables investment in cost-effective prudent contingences.

The STORM monitors the seven areas and investigates any problem or unexpected result. If there is a danger of a critical assumption becoming compromised, or if targets are not being met, an investigation is initiated to determine the cause and corrective action is implemented. It is quite normal to have redundancy built into action plans and staff can be assessed to ensure that their skills, or lack of skills, are not to blame for the plans being unsuccessful. If there are no faults in the plans or the staff, then the strategy may be the issue. The majority of non-conformance to plans are the result of staff or implementation faults rather than fundamental strategic failures, but there are times when the strategy needs to be reconsidered – for example, at strategic inflection points or when the paradigm for the business is changing.

THE BOARD'S ROLE

At the heart of the STORM model is the STORM committee, the group of individuals, usually key board members, that come together when a critical assumption (CA) appears to be in danger of becoming compromised. Utilising the ENT the likely impact of the compromised CA can be determined as well as its impact on the whole business plan. The previous scenario and real options are reviewed and, if considered robust, implemented or the criteria set for implementation should the critical assumption actually be compromised. This STORM team, with the intelligence provided by the STORM model, determine the cause of the likely compromise and specifically distinguish between staff, operational plans and strategy flaws. In the case where the objective is determined still to be sound, they can initiate the appropriate corrective action ranging from initiating staff disciplinary procedures to full revision of the corporate strategy or business plan.

STORM can be a semi-automated process, but the boss has to make the final decisions because, as this naval analogy goes:

> In naval leadership training, officers are taught that any decision that comes to the captain will not be made on facts; otherwise, it would already have been made at lower levels. So the captain's job is to make the decision on the basis of principles and to be decisive.
>
> Dean LeBaron

When the STORM necessitates a board meeting it is very likely that decisions will have to be made, as above, not on the full facts of the matter but on the available intelligence, with a degree of faith and possibly an element of fiction mixed in. This is what the board of directors are paid to do.

CHAPTER 8

BENCHMARKING PERFORMANCE

You can't manage what you can't measure.

William Hewlett

Benchmarking is considered by many to be an essential tool in a competitive market. It allows non-competitive areas to be optimised and drives down prices.

Benchmarking on the oil industries' use of computers has seen costs tumble as IT managers are able to compare the costs of running their systems with others in the industry. In areas considered to be an overhead rather than one where a competitive advantage can be gained, it is in the industries' interest to benchmark. It is less so where a company has established the area to be benchmarked as a source of some competitive advantage. Benchmarking is best at optimisation, rather than innovation, as firms with completely different ways of doing things tend not to fit well into the rigid design of benchmarking questionnaires, which tend to assume a particular way of doing things.

In order to use benchmarking effectively we have to adopt McKinsey's 7-S model (see Chapter 4, Figure 4.3) to ensure that we are looking at compatible activities and that the companies being benchmarked have a similar strategy, structure, systems, skills, shared values, staff, skills and style as our own.

Before considering benchmarking we have to ensure that we are comparing the right things: apples with apples and pears with pears. The closer the match with our company's 7-S model the better the benchmark will be and the easier any lessons learned will be to implement in our company. Therefore, we need to add something to traditional benchmarking. This new model I have called "Full Spectrum Benchmarking". It was initially developed in response to a situation that was encountered by Sun Systems Inc., in California.

On a bright sunny Californian day I was chatting to a Sun Systems executive over a coffee in the original JAVA café (where the java language was born, or so I was told). He mentioned a problem that had been encountered in their customer satisfaction benchmarking. They simply did not believe what they were seeing from a competitor's benchmarking results. Many benchmark providers mask the names of the firms you are being benchmarked against. The reported benchmark scores that their competitor was achieving appeared to be just be too high. I asked if I could see some of the benchmarking results they had been getting and using to drive their quality improvement initiatives. From the report, and my knowledge of the industry, it was clear that they were not looking at like for like. I had been visiting companies around the valley – Oracle, Compaq, Silicon Graphics, Hewlett Packard, etc. – and they all had the same problem with their benchmark provider, a well-known research firm now part of an international group. Were they comparing apples with apples? Unfortunately, the answer was "No". Sun Systems computers were being compared to Hewlett Packard printers, high-end systems with PCs, etc. In short, the research company had lost the plot. They had, I am sure unintentionally, recruited different divisions to the same benchmarking exercise. So while the results showed, for example, HP and Sun Systems customer satisfaction, the Sun Systems customer surveys were all from highly complex integrated systems, while the HP results were from consumers using HP printers only. This was clearly not a good basis for comparison.

In order to make benchmarking work you have to accept that every company is unique and will have a different 7-S summary. But like every unique chemical compound, it is made up of fundamental elements each of which produces a unique spectrum. Each part of a company – like a complex chemical compound – would contain identifiable tell-tale peaks in a spectroscopic examination. By building a picture of the company's unique spectrum, it is possible to identify common elements between companies. These common elements can be benchmarked either as "best in class" or "best in breed". The resultant research findings are perfectly compatible, and make benchmarking more reliable and, of course, valid. For example, firms may have six very different elements in their 7-S summary, but if the systems utilised by the companies are more or less the same then they can be benchmarked.

Having established that there are areas of compatibility within some aspect of the 7-S model, we then need to examine that area and build up a spectrum of its components. This can be done, in the case of Sun Systems, by considering the markets being served. In this way, high end computers sold in small numbers with high levels of support and maintenance would be at the far left of the range, while PCs sold to the home market with little support would be at the extreme right of the spectrum, with all the remaining markets featured somewhere in between.

In this way, all the major computer suppliers can be classified and a spectrum established. These spectrums can be compared and areas of overlap can clearly be benchmarked as apples are being compared with apples. Gathering benchmark data at a specific point (element) allowed a near perfect comparison to be made and the benchmarking data derived is relevant to all the participants buying into that element of comparison. This ensured that benchmarking was not distorted by product or service elements from other parts of the spectrum.

THE ABCD–WOW OF BENCHMARKING

Getting benchmarking right is important, and here are some tips on how to do it well. I call it the ABCD–WOW of benchmarking.

A – Advantages

Set objective well before we begin the exercise. Ask yourself the question: What quantifiable advantages we will derive from benchmarking? For example, successful IT supported benchmarking will reduce our IT cost by 25% within one year.

B – Best practice

While there may not be a single uniformly applicable best practice because of the unique 7-S profile of companies within an industry, has a "best practice" been described in secondary research sources? Are case studies available? There are case studies in most subject areas from designing a strategy to writing a company manual. Just because your organisation is unique does not mean that everything needs to be original. Be prepared to use as much as you can from the experiences of others. Just remember, you have to consider your uniqueness (7-S model) and particular environment before you apply the knowledge acquired.

When we start a new consultancy assignment, the first place I look is on-line and then our library. In the majority of cases I have been able to find very relevant material, ranging from case studies to entire texts addressing the very challenges I am considering. Make sure that you are not about to undertake a benchmarking exercise that has already been done and is well reported. Make sure that you are investing in obtaining knowledge that is not already documented in the industry's literature. Benchmarking is not cheap and can require a lot of internal resource or other hidden costs, so ensure that secondary research sources are reviewed first.

One of our trainee consultants was helping to design a strategy for a theatre and I asked her if she had found any books on the subject. She told me that as this was a unique theatre, she had not bothered searching. I spent 2 minutes 37 seconds on the Internet and had found, among other texts, Philip Kotler's work *Standing Room Only*. She was just about to reinvent the wheel. It is always much better to start from the most up-to-date theory and practice and develop from there. You may throw out the previous knowledge but ignorance of it is not acceptable. I tactfully suggested that she should be unique in the final solution, but make all reasonable efforts never to reinvent things.

On one assignment where we were looking at the marketing strategy of a city, my starting point was to give the client team a summary of a book on the subject. In this way, we all started from a base of the existing "best practice" or at least one person's view of best practice. This saved hours of work, allowing us to develop a breakthrough strategy that delivered for the city, generating 11,000 new jobs and attracting $252 million of inward investments.

C – Checklists

Having identified case studies and any examples of best practice you can find, the next step is to borrow or build your own checklist. I have found that a study of several best practice models can provide the material to build a robust and detailed checklist. This checklist is used in the same way that pilots use their checklists – as an aid to ensuring that all the steps in a process of getting airborne and getting down safely are undertaken, in the correct sequence, so that nothing is overlooked. The use of this checklist to compare your own business model against other models will establish obvious areas where there are internal weaknesses. These may be the priority areas for investigation during the benchmarking exercise.

As with flying, there are two basic types of checklist that can be used: the generic checklist and the specific (aircraft type) checklist. The checklist you derive from the literature and or primary research is a generic checklist. However, very few pilots would be willing to fly an aircraft with a generic checklist; they would want to have the specific checklist for the type of aircraft they are flying. There is an old flying saying: "There are old pilots and there are bold pilots, but there are no old, bold pilots." As you must know the correct take-off speed, stall speed and landing speed for your aircraft, a *specific* checklist is necessary.

The uniqueness of your organisation requires you to derive a specific checklist that will allow implementation to be achieved within your organisation. Failure to provide this tailoring may result in your stalling and crashing to the ground.

While the specific checklist is needed for safe aircraft operation, you will not be surprised to know that much of the generic checklist is the same as the specific checklist, but some critical parts will be different. This is the secret of adopting best practice – tailoring the critical parts to ensure that the system works in your organisation.

Undertake the benchmark via a reputable company, preferably one with BS EN ISO 9001, and ensure that they are comparing like with like. From this work you will quickly identify the areas where you can make improvements to your own processes and procedures. Review and implement changes but remember to consider the impact on the 7-S model. Changes in one area can impact on other areas of the 7-S model. I have found to my cost that even a single change in one area can result in major changes in another. Therefore, consider the impact of changes and anticipate reactions before implementing any changes. The larger the changes the more consideration is necessary.

D – Date stamp/revision date

Some firms are still benchmarking long after the benefits have gone. They have gained the advantages and are often continuing with the benchmarking out of habit. Once the gains have been achieved, you have to consider if it is worth continuing the practice or whether the resources would be better spent elsewhere. A date is then required to be entered into your calendar for a review of the objectives and to revise the process. Nothing lasts forever and benchmarking is no different. As I have said before, what is considered to be best practice one day is not the next. In strategic planning and operational planning, what is effective changes over time and what is possible also changes over time. Therefore, if we do not review our ideas of what is best practice we may lose ground to competitors.

Having established our best practice, having established the possible results achievable through benchmarking, and having date stamped the process, it is time to turn our attention to getting the benefits translated into the achievement of our objective. We need the WOW factor.

W – When does it work?

There is an almost childlike belief that when something works in one situation it will work in another. It is necessary to determine when best practice works and when similar practices have failed. Looking at mergers and acquisitions, why is it that some companies, like Cisco Systems, are able to acquire companies with relative ease and integrate them, almost faultlessly, not once or twice but many times each year, while some of their emulators have met with failure and reduction of shareholder value?

When a merger is successful the conditions that prevailed at the time can be determined. With the painstaking precision of a forensic scientist, you have to study the scene. Next, the elements that appear to make it successful should be separated and the actors isolated. By cross-referencing to other successful mergers, you can start to build the generic checklist of what works in certain environments.

The environment is very important as it can force mergers to work while a different environment can almost alone ensure their failure. By the environment I mean the state of the market, the industries outlook, etc.

I should now perhaps mention that it is sometimes difficult to separate the 3Fs (Fact, Faith and Fiction) in the merger stories you will read in the press and trade journals. I remember reading one that sounded great until I realised it was the same one I had been brought in to fix!

O – On what does it work?

When I say "On what does it work?" I mean what are the McKinsey's 7-S characteristics of the organisation from which the best practice example has been drawn? By doing this analysis you can develop a set of best practice models that are known to have worked in at least one specific structure. The nearer the 7-S profile of our company is to that of the other company, the more likely it can be transferred successfully. Each element of the 7-S model can likewise be compared, and again the closer the individual element is to what you see in the other organisation, the higher the probability of obtaining similar success in our company by adopting the practice.

In the example of the merger, each of the companies involved needs to be assessed to determine the profiles that are more likely to succeed. There is no real surprise here that the closer the company gets to the 7-S characteristics, the less problematic the merger. Hence, in mature industries where companies are similar, they can be merged relatively easily and with little risk. The greater the differences, the greater the merger challenges.

W – Why does it work?

You will remember this question WHY? WHY? WHY? This is a drill-down question. You have to establish, without any shadow of a doubt, why the particular examples you are studying worked. There are never perfect answers unfortunately, but you have to develop your own theory and, if possible, verify it. By developing a theory, listing the critical assumptions and then testing and/or monitoring implementation, you will be able to refine the why and develop a specific implementation checklist for your organisation.

Research

From the "ABCD–WOW" you will have gathered that there is a substantial amount of research involved in producing a successful implementation of market leading processes and procedures. However, the research does not end there. You will need to test and monitor performance against your expectation. Deviations from expectation should be explored and corrected by improving implementation or by redesigning the module. It is easier and faster to correct a small deviation from expectations than to allow things to get so far from targets that major changes are required. Therefore, close monitoring is required, especially in the early stages of the change management process.

PROJECT PLANNING

The typical development time for a successful benchmark or best practice integration is three months and will involve a team of three people: two full-time and one in a supervisory capacity. Well, when I say supervisory, perhaps I mean "devil's advocate" role. It is essential to challenge thinking and ensure research quality if improvements are going to have any chance of working, but remember, do not try to allow for every eventuality, the most common 80% of eventualities is sufficient to start with.

The planning process requires the following steps:

- Review of existing knowledge.
- Identification of research candidates potentially exhibiting best practice.
- Screening, using primary research/benchmarking of these candidates to determine the 3Fs of their claims of best practice.
- Primary research around the case studies aimed at determining:
  - the 7-S of the organisations involved;
  - the publics involved and the balance of their relationships;
  - the market, social, organisational, economic, political or relevant environment.
- Formulation of the generic checklists.
- Examination of your own organisation to determine the fit.
- Tailoring of the generic checklist to the specific checklist.
- Documenting the rational and drawing out the critical assumptions made.

- Determine the other areas in the 7-S model that will be likely to require changes, and anticipate any issues that require to be addressed before implementation.
- Testing and or monitoring programme developed and assigned.
- Pilot if possible.
- Launch the change management programme.
- Date stamp for review.

Each of these stages will take more time or less time, depending on the size and nature of the changes required. There is always a risk in change management and before first investigating the consequences of the compromise in the STORM process described earlier, you should never blindly persist in implementing changes when indicators are suggesting that the critical assumptions on which it is based, are becoming compromised.

SUMMARY

- Benchmarking can be very beneficial.
- You must compare apples with apples.
- The 7-S model is required to judge the ease of adoption of any new practices discovered.
- The environment has a significant impact on what works when, and any differences between that and your current environment may impact your success.

CHAPTER 9

CORPORATE SYSTEMS TO AID MANAGEMENT AND CONTROL

So much of what we call management consists in making it difficult for people to work.

Peter Drucker

I have already mentioned the issues there are around compliance, and the need to have a view of the whole organisation has never been more important. Thankfully, computers and the software that run them have risen to the challenge and there are several, almost essential, tools that the marketing director needs to be familiar with and understand their potential. Clearly the size of the company will dictate the packages that you can afford or indeed will be useful. However, I have seen Enterprise Resource Planning (ERP) packages at Microsoft office prices, and some advanced systems such as Customer Relationship Management (CRM) tools being given away with books in the single user version. So even small companies can have some very sophisticated tools, but I do not recommend introducing unnecessary complexity. If all you need is a spreadsheet, then settle for that, but if you foresee rapid growth, then acquire as soon as possible all the tools you expect to need. To try to tackle new systems in a major growth spurt can stall a company, so plan for growth by using as many "On Demand" services as possible.

"On Demand" is available from Oracle, Microsoft and others and in most areas, including ERP, CRM, sales force management, etc., they allow your organisation to grow rapidly without any significant danger of IT failures.

ON DEMAND

"On Demand" is a fast growing market sector which, for rapid growth companies, offers some advantages over the traditional software-purchasing route. You hire the software and hardware that runs it remotely, and all you need is a computer with internet access. You can have one user or 100 users, so as the company grows you simply add new users, with no need to upgrade systems or worry about secure maintenance, etc., as it's all taken care of. Of course, all this flexibility comes at a cost but compared to the cost of getting the growth phase wrong it is relatively good value.

Like all things, "On Demand" has a few drawbacks not least of which is your willingness to put your trust in a third party, and have your customer details, accounts, financial records, etc., on someone else's server. You have to be able to trust your provider. Several commentators have cast dispersions on TPV (Third Party Vendors) and their honesty in reporting their activity, ranging from the quality of sales leads they generated, the call quality and the number of irregularities, to computer down time and problem resolution.

Phil Wainwright on DZ net proposed a code of conduct for "On Demand" providers:

- Say exactly what the contract does and does not deliver.
- Spell out what to do if something does go wrong.
- Report live service level metrics.
- Let customers download their data whenever they like.
- Accept 30 days' notice of termination at any time, no questions asked.

So, before entering into any agreement, discover how many of these points apply to your vendor.

In 2007, Nucleus Research reported in their US study that 75% of companies with over 1,000 employees were using some form of "On Demand Solution", while McKinsey Research in 2006 reported that 61% of chief information officers (CIOs) were considering some form of Software as a Service (SaaS) application. (On Demand and SaaS are different terms for more or less the same service.) Incidentally, the SaaS/On Demand market is estimated to be worth at least $10 billion.

The leading SaaS/On Demand applications are in:

- Web-conferencing and collaboration.
- Human resource and payroll.
- CRM and sales force management.
- Supply chain and purchasing management, including invoice and payment.
- Web content management, e-mail, e-mail marketing, e-commerce.
- Financial and business administration, including ERP.
- Market research/customer satisfaction monitoring and reporting.

Firms of all sizes are reported to be embracing the On Demand technology or considering how it can be employed. Its role in marketing and marketing research should be considered, but all issues should be explored before choosing either to adopt this new approach or to continue with the traditional methods of software and system administration.

The principal software tools of interest to the marketing director are those directly related to marketing, including sales, and those related to management and control. Below I have listed some of the software that you may find useful.

Within the marketing area we can see the need for tools to help with:

- Organising marketing activities
- Monitoring critical assumptions
- Communications
- Handling remote workers
- Expenses and budgets
- Staff and personnel management, including KRAs (key result areas)
- Market intelligence dissemination
- Multidisciplinary team management
- Calendars and diaries
- New product development
- Pricing
- Customer service
- Customer satisfaction and loyalty
- Market modelling
- Task management

RELATIONSHIP SYSTEMS

The best-known applications at the corporate marketing level are:

- Customer Relationship Management
- Enterprise Resource Planning

- Balanced Scorecard and other dashboard applications
- Mind mapping software
- Scenario planning software
- Market research and customer satisfaction reporting

Customer Relationship Management

Customer Relationship Management (CRM) tools are available from a variety of providers from the market leader SAP to On Demand/SaaS providers such as Salesforce.com.

CRM is a system that gives a complete overview of the client/company exchange. The system involves itself in every means of communication and exchange between the organisation and the customer. A CRM program is customised to effectively meet the needs of any individual organisation's customer requirements.

Individuals who experience a beneficial exchange with a business are commonly more faithful and lucrative. Taking into account that, in most businesses, the cost of obtaining a new customer usually exceeds the cost of retaining a present client, investing in a process that keeps your customers has obvious benefits for the company. Sizeable organisations may expend vast sums of money on a CRM system. In order for CRM to be effective it must be tailored to an organisation's requirements and this is where most vendors make their money. If you are not clear on what you need, then it is going to be a long, painful and expensive process.

The acronym CRM was initially applied by companies that produced and sold sales force automation (SFA) software. These are robust pieces of software used by sales teams to control daily communications with clients. The sales teams log all they know about the client, note all communications, and describe the outcome of every meeting into the SFA software. In addition, they plan follow-on activities to the sale, and the application notifies them when those actions should be carried out. These applications can connect to databases within businesses in order to draw out previous financial transactions, product utilisation, remittance history, as well as additional knowledge that assists the sales team in maximising their relationship with the client. These applications allow managers to assess what each member of the sales team is working on and how efficiently they are utilising their time.

SFA technologies are important in the process but they represent only a section of it. The technology encompasses:

- Databases
- Strategies
- Campaign planning
- Complex statistical analysis
- Effective communication
- Timely and widespread application.

The advantages that can be gained by employing a high-quality CRM system include:

- Increased customer retention
- Improved levels of client loyalty
- Maximisation of profit from present client base
- Increased company recognition.

It is interesting to note that some very large CRM implementations have fallen far short of achieving many of the above. So caution and a great deal of care in planning are required to ensure that implementation works. Don't forget that the 7-S model changing systems and processes will impact staff, etc., so ensure that you engage them in the change process.

Enterprise Resource Planning

An Enterprise Resource Planning (ERP) system involves the consolidation of all units and operations across an organisation into an individual computer application that can assist specific needs and enable contact within the organisation, as well as the common use of data that is produced by the application.

The term "enterprise resource planning" was derived by the Gartner Group in the 1990s, and involved the integration of the main company software applications. The group determined that these applications had to encompass combined elements for accounts, financial matters, sales and distribution, human resources, materials control, and various corporate operations, and the system foundation would be used across the entire organisation. This definition involves three fundamental components:

1. ERP applications are versatile in range, covering various functions including economic effects, proposals, purchasing, construction and personnel.
2. ERP applications are consolidated and involve data being entered into a certain operation, thus data in all connected units is also transformed instantly.
3. ERP applications are composed of modules and are therefore applicable in any amalgamation of the modules.

Global ERP application companies, including SAP-AG, Oracle, J.D. Edwards and Baan, have a share of about three-quarters of the ERP market.

An ERP system can be assembled in a number of ways, including the deployment of software from a single supplier. In other circumstances, the company can install various components from a number of suppliers. Both methods have their own advantages and disadvantages. Using various modules can offer the best functionality for each module, but installing them can be particularly difficult due to certain boundaries that need to be created. A single supplier application may not have all the functionality required, but it can be simpler to install. Even though numerous global organisations have installed ERP applications, most of them have implemented them towards the end of the 1990s and are almost due for renewal. Despite this, there is mixed evidence regarding their usefulness – from firms who have made them mission critical and swear by them, to others who have been forced to abandon a vision of a totally integrated company, and are accepting a lesser vision. These ERP applications can be hit or miss, and as the market's experience is mixed, there is a lack of information on relating to the installation, functionality or outcome. Information on ERP effectiveness is sometimes conflicting and often clearly distorted to fit a particular story.

There are four major reasons why companies undertake ERP implementations:

1. Consolidation of financial information.
2. Homogenisation of operations.
3. Streamlining of human resources data.
4. Integration of marketing with financial data.

Balanced Scorecard and other dashboard applications

These applications are used to give management an overview of their company's performance against its stated goals and are now deployed in some form in most of the world's largest companies.

Dashboards are best when they are capable of being interrogated to determine the cause of any failure to meet expectations, and the nearer to real-time/right-time they are the better. Like all intelligence systems they need to be built on irrefutable data. This simple necessity is often missed on some very sophisticated systems, and the old computer adage comes to mind: "garbage in, garbage out".

Mind mapping software

There are many tools now available to help in the creative process and two I recommend are mind mapping and hexagonal thinking tools.

Mind mapping tools are available from a number of sources and a Google search will find many providers, including free software such as "Freemind" as well as easy to order packages from Visual Mind and Nova Mind. Although I am told that in South American Spanish "no va" – meaning "does not go" – is perhaps not the best name for the creative thinking tool.

Tony Buzan is the father of mind mapping and if you have not read his work *Use your Brain* then rush out and buy it now. It is guaranteed to help you in many of your new tasks as a marketing director.

Scenario planning software

Scenario planning has become more and more important in the strategic planning process since one of its leading exponents, Arie de Geus, published his book *The Living Company*. There are also Idon's software and the concepts discussed in Miriam Galt *et al.*'s book *Idon Scenario Thinking*. By combining Idon's software and methodology with business intelligence, the power of the scenarios is enhanced and you will be spellbound not only by the creative thinking that is forthcoming but also by how much fun scenario planning can be. That is not to say it should be taken lightly, as it is a very powerful tool for dealing with uncertainty.

The fundamental benefit of scenario planning is that, as situations change, decisions can be made extremely quickly as the outcome modelling has already been done for the majority of stages. This model also helps strategists to record and monitor strategic implementation, assessing the success of various scenarios for future reference.

Scenario planning, utilising the hexagonal thinking model, allows a very pragmatic view of the future by distilling it down into a series of "what if" options and classifying these by their probability of occurrence. Then taking the two extremes of "happens" or "does not happen" from this and the subsequent trees of events, it is possible to derive the best and worst scenarios. Having strategies to cope with both extremes allows the actual position to be addressed effectively, whatever comes to pass.

The Idon scenario impact matrix is then used to derive the decision options, differentiated competences and develop robust options for taking the appropriate action. The derivation of the differentiated competences effectively produces the unique proposition that will be required to be successful given any particular scenario.

This Idon modelling ensures that essential actions continue to be carried out; that actions that you may have to take in the short term are dropped at the appropriate time; and that actions you may have to prepare to undertake are developed. In addition, you are alerted to the possible impact, both favourable and unfavourable, of the actions being considered. All this allows the identification of the future core competences and the capabilities required under the various scenarios. Thus, competitive advantage can be gained and maintained even in an uncertain future.

Idon software also provides methods of priority modelling, option mapping, goal navigation modelling, process modelling, system thinking, dilemma modelling and creative modelling. This provides a platform for a complete range of scenario and strategic modelling exercises. All of this software has a role to play in developing strategic direction and clarifying your organisation's senior management's thinking.

The advantage of the software-based system is that various stages in the thinking process can be saved and a track record is obtained. In this way, when a critical assumption is compromised and a review of strategy is required, the exact steps utilised by the strategy team in the previous scenario planning process can be retraced. This allows the team to pick up from the point at which the compromised critical assumption was used, saving considerable time and allowing managers to very quickly retrace the logic root they were following during the strategic planning session.

This ability to fit back into the active mindset of the previous strategy session has two advantages: it can expose other, less obvious, errors in the previous logic and ensures that the strategy correction is not out of context in the wider strategy picture. If the original mindset is not re-established, it is remarkably easy for the strategy team to go off at a tangent in seeking a solution to the emerging issue. If this is allowed to occur, the resultant modification will be out of tune with the rest of the corporate strategy and long-term mission. A quick run through of the series of models previously derived (a storyboard) has an almost NLP (Neuro Linguistic Programming) effect of bringing the participants' minds back into the previous mindset. This is essential for a consistent approach to strategy planning where there has been a time interval or even personnel changes.

Where there have been personnel changes, I have found that, while the new participants may not wholly share the views of the original strategy team, they at least understand how the view was derived and the logic that was followed. This allows their questions to be answered quickly and for them to either agree the logic of the old model or highlight errors that, in context, others can agree were wrong or can convince the newcomers of their validity.

The ability to save various visuals of the strategy development, at important points in the development process, is one of the fastest ways of reminding the strategy team how they reached the original strategy. A similar technique can be employed in advertising where, after an initial long advert has been broadcast, it is possible to have the audience recall the whole advert just by showing highlights in subsequent promotions. Strategy model capture is a fast recall mechanism for strategic planners, which does not delay the initial strategic process.

Market simulation modelling

Using various marketing modelling tools, this system models the markets you are operating within. This includes the standard market models such as: Ansoff matrix, Boston matrix, Directional Policy matrix, Income/Profit Gap analysis, Market Share analysis, perceptual mapping, Risk analysis, SWOT analysis and market mapping.

This visual right-time system allows a clear and accurate picture to be presented of your market. It is extremely valuable in simulation exercises where the effects of various scenarios can be modelled in terms of market perception, income gaps, etc. This helps by enhancing the image of the future scenario and shows the issues that are likely to be generated from the impact on the market.

These models are useful in day-to-day operation and can be linked to real-time market data such as that produced by omnibus or panel research. This overtime provides a lapsed photography-type model of the market as it grows and develops. These can be represented on websites and you can look back using our Dynamic Insight modules to see how the market has changed over the time of study in which you are interested.

As well as the dynamic market simulations and models, we are developing internal models that map the internal alignment of the organisation. This modelling tool will allow you to see how the internal environment is moving and enable you to compare this to the environment required by the strategy.

Both internal and external mapping require access to market intelligence and are only as real as the data provided. In some cases, where the data is very difficult to acquire or is simply not available, these models and simulations are subject to the 3Fs. The more unreliable or infrequent the data, the more it tends to move away from Fact and towards Faith and ultimately Fiction. These models are excellent when you have invested in rich data but can be misleading where an investment in quality data has not been made.

Market research and customer satisfaction reporting

One of the best SaaS products on the market is Dynamic Insight provided by MMSI. Oh, that's my company and perhaps I am a little biased here; so don't listen to me, just read what users have said about it:

> The "dynamic" element makes it possible to see what's happening before it is too late to take action.

> The ability to track down soft skills of specific employees and the ability to check for results by product line.

> It provides the motivation and feedback to control and improve the quality of our services.

> Fast, reliable and stable.

Some 93.87% of those users surveyed thought that Dynamic Insight was user friendly, and with an availability better than 99.98%, it is a very stable service.

Dynamic Insight is the latest generation of the "On Demand" research reporting tool, which has been in use on a global scale since 2002. Dynamic Insight was released in 2006 and incorporates a revision of the previous "Dynamic Reporting" that has increased the response time of the application, the range of functions, the range of outputs available to the user, and created a modular application that can be easily modified for individual clients as they desire.

Benefits

- Derived variables for significance testing and deltas (variances).
- Presentation of insights into corrective actions from known environmental conditions and attempted solutions.
- Fully automated.
- Canned or production report tailored to individual stakeholder requirements.

Advanced features

- Flexible output graphs and tables easily importable into Microsoft Office and most other major productivity applications.
- Data can be exported in HTML, CSV and Excel formats.
- Include data/results from multiple sources.
- Modular design allowing easy customisation to different client requirements/needs.

Overview

Dynamic Insight is hugely flexible in its presentation and content capabilities. Employing the latest in AJAX design, Dynamic Insight can interface with multiple databases providing a user friendly front end to the data displaying it according to assigned permissions in attractive tables and graphs. The use of permissions allows administrators to block access to data on a user by user role, allowing users to only see reports as permitted and only see data relevant to their partner/site or business unit, although permissions may be assigned by any field within the data, and are restrictive rather than permissive so that permission to see data is given rather than denied. Dynamic Insight also provides a secure file store so that files may be shared among users, but can be restricted to specific groups of users.

Partner/site/business unit reports

Depending on the user community, dashboard(s) can be configured to contain only top-level scores, or provide additional levels of information and detail by partner and site. Dynamic Insight reports are password protected by user group.

Statistics

Dynamic Insight is capable of producing statistics and significance testing with the calculations being totally customisable by project or client, allowing it to provide clear and relevant data for the specific client.

Graphs

Dynamic Insight includes a Flash based graphing engine, which can generate a variety of graphs, which will clearly scale to the resolution of the user's display.

The following chart options are available:

- Time series graphs.
- Impact chart (prioritises action areas by presenting all attributes on one graph with correlations, attribute scores and overall satisfaction scores). This is visually a very high impact tool.
- Histograms, bar charts, pie charts, parallel column charts and line charts are all available.

Tailored to unique requirements

Dynamic Insight is designed in a modular fashion, allowing extra functions to be designed and plugged into the main menu seamlessly.

SUMMARY

- Software is available to support the marketing function.
- On Demand or SaaS appear to be gaining acceptance and are essential for rapid growth in firms.
- CRM, ERP, and other tools are almost a necessity for companies to be able to run an effective marketing operation.
- New corporate-wide systems are not without deployment risk and considerable care needs to be taken to ensure a successful implementation.
- Creative tools as well as scenario planning aids and research reporting tools are a great boost to productivity.

CHAPTER 10

BOARDROOM POLITICS: "ONLY THE PARANOID SURVIVE"

I attribute Intel's ability to sustain success to being constantly on the alert for threats, either technological or competitive in nature. The word paranoia is meant to suggest that attitude, an attitude that constantly looks over the horizon for threats to your success.

Andy Grove, chairman of Intel

If you have not already read Machiavelli's *The Prince* do so now; if you have read it some time ago then re-read it. For those who find it difficult there are many guides to Machiavelli; in a business context try Stanley Bing's book *What Would Machiavelli Do?* subtitled *The Ends Justify the Means.*

The reason I bring Machiavelli to your attention is not to have you emulate his vision for the Prince but rather to ensure that you can recognise the techniques and can defend yourself against others who may adhere to the cries of "the ends justify the means". If we are to ensure that the company succeeds, we need to make it market oriented and gain wide board approval for its position as the most important function in the company.

BOARDROOM THREATS

There are two major groups of threat to you and the good of the organisation, they are: internal and external.

Internal or external threats come from a variety of sources and may be motivated by a number of things.

Internal

- When a personal ambition conflicts with company good.
- Paradigm shift can mean that the board become ineffective and afraid to take the action necessary to correct the situation until it's too late.
- Fraud, theft or embezzlement.
- Poor management.
- Subordinate judgement.

External

- Competitors' actions.
- Market changes.
- Bad luck.
- Accidents or bad PR.
- Suppliers failing to deliver on promises.

KNOWLEDGE IS POWER

How can you see a problem coming and prevent it from damaging the company?

As the marketing director you will be responsible for marketing intelligence and hence be the oracle of knowledge. If you can't detect any changes in the market, no one else will.

So far we have been dealing with the practical aspects of running a first-class board. However, the reality is that in many boards, especially in small and family-run businesses, there are, sad to say, some whose best interests appear not to be aligned with the company. These individuals can destroy a company by forcing out the best talent and actively sideroad anyone who disagrees with their specific point of view, be it right or wrong.

In my experience the power struggles of boards are inversely proportional to the success of the company. That is to say, the more politics, the smaller and less significant the company, or at least it soon will be. Perhaps it is a result rather than a common trait. If there are boardroom problems, the company can quickly fall apart.

I remember working in a small company and one of the board meetings actually resulted in a physical fight between the managing director and a fellow director over who was giving most of their time to the company. On more than one occasion I have been attending family board meetings where nothing could get done because of the in-fighting or the patriarch completely living in the past and not being willing to accept that unless changes were going to be made soon there would be no business.

I am not arguing against dictatorships or for open democracy in the boardroom. Some companies have been run highly successfully by near dictators, but like all dictatorships they tend to fall with a crash in the end. On the other scale, is the liberal democracy that turns into a farce in a crisis and the business can be destroyed by indecision and over-analysis. As Darrell Huff in *How to Lie with Statistics* wrote: "If you torture the data long enough, it will confess to anything."

Somewhere between these two extremes lies the perfect company that has not only a strong leader but also a strong board that, before a decision is made, speak their minds freely and without fear, and will all pull together behind the leader when a decision is reached. If you like the price of open democracy in the boardroom, it is an external show of complete solidarity.

There has been a lot of discussion on the topic of power, and by far the most famous work in this area is Machiavelli's *The Prince*. Nicolò de Bernardo dei Machiavelli was born in the city-state of Florence on the 3rd of May 1527. He is credited with writing the "bible" on how to gain and maintain power. He points out "Force and prudence, then, are the might of all the governments" and this also holds true for boards of directors.

His work points out to the would-be "Prince" how to gain power, and is famously misquoted as suggesting the "ends justify the means". While the work points out how to gain and maintain power, it does not pass comment on the morality of what is required, but only reports on what works. Therefore it is essential that you have a good grasp of the book to enable you to see and understand what others may be trying to do to gain power. Here are a few business context translations of *The Prince*, but I feel the original work is the best.

I have seen, at first hand, some of the Machiavellian techniques used very effectively. I remember a college merger where three distinct colleges were to be merged under one united banner. As the three rural colleges had strong identity and loyal structures, this was not going to be an easy task. The colleges saw themselves as three individual colleges running their own systems and were not going to willingly be forced together. The Principal, knowing he had to create a new united loyalty structure, had to first destroy the strong bonds of loyalty that staff felt in each college to their superiors. He first introduce a matrix management system, knowing that the side effect would initially create some confusion in the established chain of command and generate a degree of insecurity and back stabbing. He then asked everyone to apply for their old jobs or one of the new matrix-generated posts. Then, at the first opportunity, he promoted a lecturer to a vice principal post, bypassing the heads of department and the normal step-by-step, dead-man's-shoes type promotion to which the colleges had been accustomed. Suddenly anyone could get any job, was the impression. Overnight all the old loyalties were destroyed as subordinates applied for the jobs of their bosses. It was a masterstroke, and pure Machiavelli. The Principal now constructed a new hierarchy by moving promoted or reappointed staff from one college to another. These individuals owed their position to one person only, the Principal, and they knew it; and the fact that they were in a new, often hostile, environment galvanised their support for his policies.

Needless to say, he made a lot of enemies in the process, but as Carl Icahn, a notorious corporate raider put it: "In the takeover business, if you want a friend, you buy a dog." In less than one year the Principal had achieved an almost impossible task of creating one united college from three strongly independent colleges.

There is no question in my mind that the techniques proposed by Machiavelli are effective, and if they had been followed in the Iraq war there would be a lot less violence there now. According to Machiavelli, a dictatorship is the easiest to topple and in which to substitute a new order. Perhaps George Bush and Tony Blair did not read Machiavelli or there is another plot we are not yet aware of.

Machiavelli is not to be followed literally and his suggestions do not fit well into modern standards of decency and morality. For example, the killing of the old marketing director's family and key supporters could land you in a lot of trouble these days.

The reality is that there is a lot of politics and you have to acquire the skills necessary to survive and defend yourself from games played by others less interested in the company and more interested in themselves.

STANDARD PROTECTION MECHANISMS

- Keep all e-mails.
- Confirm verbal agreements in writing.

- Do not speak badly of or be in the company of others speaking badly of fellow members of the board.
- Be above reproach in your conduct of business.
- Be seen to be honest, dependable and trustworthy.

Unfortunately it is not enough to be honest, dependable and trustworthy, you must also be seen to be. It is often the simple things that are noted, e.g. buy a stamp for a personal letter, be seen to use a call box for a private call, etc. The effects of your actions are magnified by the size of the company, so if you make a publicly observed private call do the staff assume that it's OK for everyone to spend 50% of the day on private calls?

The perfect combination of force and prudence is the best way to survive a politically motivated boardroom.

RISK TAKERS

As Harold Macmillan said: "To be alive at all involves some risk." I have found that entrepreneurial companies are mostly led by risk takers. These leaders take calculated risks but how are the risks calculated? Many of the leaders are high flyers and made it to the top by taking risks.

The problem you will often encounter with high flyers is that they are predominantly risk takers even when it's not necessary. If you follow Darwin, you would have thought that this would have been bred out of business by now if it was a bad trait. If it is a good trait, then how do we reconcile it with Machiavelli's requirement for prudence? Prudence is defined as the act of being prudent, which in turn is defined as: Being wise in the handling of practical matters, exercising good judgement, or common sense. Synonyms are careful, wise and responsible.

These traits of prudence are not necessarily incompatible with taking a calculated risk, and as there are no rewards without some risk I could argue that, therefore, taking business risks is very prudent in the business sense. However, research in psychology has revealed that human perceptions of risk vary enormously. It may come as no surprise that a high sensation seeker, such as a sky-diver, appraise risk differently from non-extreme sport partici-pants. The extreme sport participant tends to dramatically underestimate risk.

It would appear that when appraising risk those who enjoy extreme sports envisage a degree of pleasure in the achievement of the task, while others see only pain. The contemplation of pleasure causes the brain to release serotonin – a mood-enhancing hormone – which makes the risk appear to be less daunting and more of a challenge. The serotonin-soaked brain's perception of the world is different from others, especially those who perceive pain rather than pleasure. They perceive greater risk in the same activity.

In some companies this can be taken to an extreme where the founder increasingly takes bigger and bigger risks, endangering the company. The Greeks knew this as *akrasia*, "an impulse towards self-destruction". Many individuals achieve greatness only to throw it all away on a stupid risk. Your company must ensure that risks are managed by clear heads and that *akrasia* is avoided.

The work of Frank Farley (1990) in studying extreme athletes concluded that propensity to risk was biological. He defined Big T (T standing for thrill seekers) as people who prefer uncertainty, novelty, high risk, ambiguity and low structure. These individuals often see the world differently, are highly driven, and they often change the world with their ideas and inventions. As part of the board they can make your company great, but can also destroy it. Balance is the answer: being able to manage the huge potential of Big T types without risking everything.

Managing Big T types is not easy as there is some negativity to their behaviour. According to Farley, they are prone to addiction, including drugs, alcohol, gambling, suicidal behaviour and promiscuity. As it is the risk and thrill they strive for, you have to be careful to ensure they are channelled in the right direction and that they are constructively utilising their unique talents for the benefit of the organisation.

Perhaps one of the best descriptions I read was:

> . . . extreme introverts, yet they view social status as being impor-
> tant but mainly derive satisfaction from personal achievement rather
> than social approval. They enjoy the spotlight and seek activities
> that reinforce status and while being part of a group are strongly
> self-sufficient. They are therefore ambitious, organised and tena-
> cious. They plan ahead and have due concern for detail, while they
> tend towards exhibitionism and the unconventional. They are very
> critical of all authority apart from their own; they are highly opin-
> ionated and do not readily accept challenges to their opinions. They
> are driven to be successful and to accomplish something of
> significance.

(I have just had a frightening thought; the above horoscope could be describing me!)

While they can be charismatic leaders they tend to make bad managers because of their reluctance to accept contradictory opinions.

So we have a dilemma. We need to take risks to be successful, but too great a risk could end in disaster, while force and prudence make the best long-term strategy. Those capable of seeing the world differently, and hence generating the next paradigm shift, can't see all the risks and tend to take things too far if left to their own devices. What is needed is balance and a way of measuring risk effectively so that even the Big T types can see the real risk. We need a method of separating Fact from Faith from Fiction, of determining when we are in danger of making type 1 or type 2 errors, and of ensuring that the board's perceptions of the environment are real.

Making errors from hypotheses

Type 1 error occurs when we reject a hypothesis that is in fact true, while type 2 error is when we accept as true a hypothesis that is in fact false (see Figure 10.1).

Is flying destroying the environment? If we accept this hypothesis then we may choose not to fly, but this decision could be vulnerable to type 2 error; on the other hand, if we reject the hypothesis we run the risk of type 1 error. In order to avoid both types of error we need to ensure that we have irrefutable DIKI. Listening to the news and hearing a message repeated may give the illusion of it being true, but that is also the basis of good propaganda, which is not considered by many to be necessarily true. We have to consider several factors in our determination of whether the statement or hypothesis is true or false. We have to consider:

• What is the balance of expert opinion?
• What is the depth of feeling on the subject?
• Does implicit knowledge support the hypothesis or not?
• Is there explicit data or information to support the hypothesis?
• What is the degree of correlation of the data within individual studies?

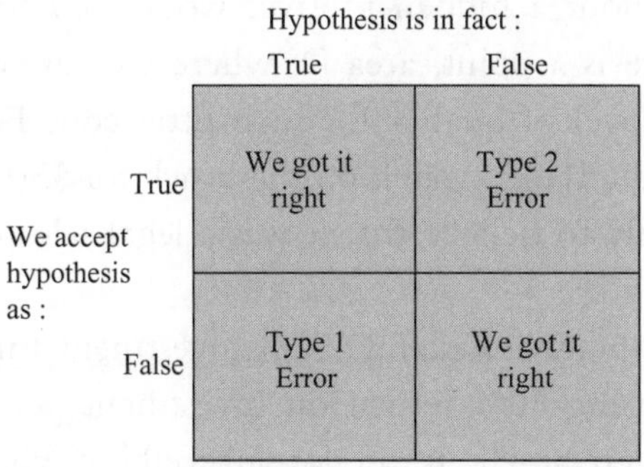

Hypothesis is in fact :

		True	False
We accept hypothesis as :	True	We got it right	Type 2 Error
	False	Type 1 Error	We got it right

Figure 10.1 Type 1 and Type 2 errors

- What is the correlation between different studies on the same topic?

A good check on reality is to also ask:

- Does this make common sense?
- Is it logical?
- Do I feel lucky?

Believability curve

There is also a believability barrier that has to be understood. We are all willing to accept certain things as true: For example, the higher the price the better the quality. We find it hard to believe that something can be of very high quality and have a very low price.

In Figure 10.2 I have prepared a believability diagram that was described to me by Professor Baker, who has now retired from Strathclyde University. We can see that in area A we can accept quite easily that a high-quality item will be expensive; likewise, we can accept in area B that a cheap item will be of low quality. We can define low quality and high price as "rip off" and, beyond that, area C as unbelievable. For example, no one in his right mind and without a hidden motive, would pay $5 for $1 note. Likewise, there is a point, area D, where we cannot believe you can buy that level of quality for such little cost. For example, if you are offered a Rolex watch on the beach for $50.00 you would be very unlikely to believe that it was a legal sale of a real Rolex – even if it was.

In a more practical example, an investment fund launched a product promising 10% return on investment per annum when interest rates were at 4%. It did not sell well but when the product was re-launched promising only an 8% return, it was over sub-

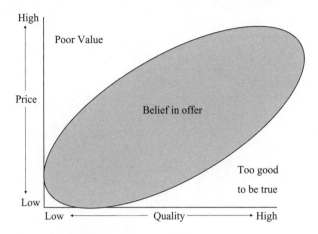

Figure 10.2 Believability curve

scribed. The 10% promise fell outside the safe investment believability curve of the independent financial advisers who sold the
product on, and they suspected higher attached risk than they did
with the same product promising only an 8% return. Clearly we
want to be able to look beyond a habitual believability curve and
establish what is actually possible and what is not. We need to be
able to construct reality curves.

SUMMARY

- Paranoia and believability curves abound in the boardroom.
- To gain credibility you must be seen to be credible.
- Spin is in, but delivery on your promises is critical if you are
  to retain your illustrious board position.

CHAPTER 11

THE STOCK MARKET

THE ROLE OF FINANCE

While it is very probable that there will be a finance director in your company, in your role as a director you should have a good grasp of how to read the accounts and be able to detect when things are not quite right.

The basic role of finance is to provide funds when they are required. The company may need to buy equipment that will generate income over time but which may cost more than the firm's current income. The company needs to fund the equipment to benefit from the future income stream that it will generate. There are four basic options open to the company:

1. To borrow the money from the bank.
2. To lease the equipment.

3. To use funds generated from previous profits that have been retained.

4. To use shareholders' funds.

The bank and leasing company will charge interest while the shareholders will be looking for a dividend or share value growth.

The issue to consider when making the decision of which finance option to choose is to ensure that the company has sufficient liquidity to meet its foreseen and perhaps unforeseen short-term money requirements. Should it not be able to meet its short-term financial requirements, the company may be considered insolvent. Insolvency is related primarily to cash flow and not necessarily to profitability. A profitable firm can become insolvent just as quickly as a non-profitable company, although it is not as inevitable as the insolvency of a non-profitable company.

The consequences of insolvency are that the company may be put into receivership by its creditors and its assets may be sold to meet its debts. This is rarely a satisfactory situation for the company or its creditors as creditors will rarely recover their money to any great extent.

Some naïve managers think that, given the balance sheet, voluntary liquidation will meet the creditors' demands for payment. In my experience, when a company is in liquidation its asset value evaporates and the vultures pick over the corporate carcass leaving very little to show of the perceived company value. Restructuring and renegotiating the debt are much better options in these unwelcome situations. Liquidation is a last resort when all else has failed.

The moral of the story is: In bad times talk most to your creditors, keep them informed, and provide them with some glimmer of hope of recovering their money if they resist the temptation to call in the liquidators. Experienced suppliers will have been through the process before and know that there is little to gain, while inexperienced suppliers will be about to find out.

Cash flow is simply money in versus money out, with consideration to monetary reserves. More important than any other report you will see as a board director is the cash flow statement. Study it carefully and ensure that there will always be funds to meet short-term creditors. You can only reap long-term profits if you survive to see the long term, therefore ensure that short-term cash flow needs are secure.

SHAREHOLDERS

Shareholders are looking for one or both of the following: The expectation of being paid a dividend and/or increased capital growth. This capital growth is based on the appreciation of the share price and this, in turn, is normally dependent on increasing profits and/or dividend growth. In both cases the main aim is an increase in the real or perceived future profits of the company. There is no gain without pain, and the pain side of the equation is the risk the investor is taking. It is normal to expect a higher reward for taking a bigger risk, and less risky investments usually attract lower returns. If we consider the bank to represent low risk, then the return we get from the bank is the base line against which investors will measure investment opportunities. A company will be expected to return more than a bank if there is any risk attached to owning the shares.

PROFIT AND LOSS ACCOUNTS AND BALANCE SHEETS

Every quoted company registered in the UK is required by law to provide its shareholders with a point in time view of how well the company is performing. The published accounts consisting of both the balance sheet and the profit and loss account provide this moment in time snapshot of the company's performance.

The profit and loss account

Looking at the profit and loss account, it can be observed that it is broken into three parts:

*   The trading account
*   The profit and loss account
*   The appropriations account.

The trading account

This is simply a statement of the total revenue less operating expenses. Put simply, the sales less the cost of sales, and the sum of these figures is known as the trading profit/loss or gross income.

The profit and loss account

This part of the statement sums up all the other expenses that are incurred by the company, and when subtracted from the gross profit provided in the trading account they generate the net profit/ loss before tax.

The appropriations account

This part of the statement shows how the company has used the new profit (after tax). For example, the company may have retained the profit, or provided shareholders with a dividend.

Trading Account

Sales	280,000	
Cost of sales	120,000	
Net profit		160,000

Profit and Loss Account

Auditors' fees	5,000	
Depreciation	10,000	
Insurance	3,000	
Consultancy fees	2,000	
Net profit before tax		140,000
Corporation tax	28,000	
Net profit after tax		112,000

Appropriations Account

Ordinary share dividend	12,000	
To reserve		100,000

The balance sheet

The second part of the financial statement provided to share-holders is the balance sheet. The balance sheet is split into four sections:

- Liabilities
- Current liabilities
- Fixed assets
- Current assets.

The term "current " refers to items that are turned over quickly; for example, stock, material used in production, cash. A typical balance sheet would look like this:

Liabilities
Share capital
Issued 100,000 ordinary   100,000
  shares at 1 GBP
Retained earnings   200,000
Total   300,000

Current liabilities
Creditors   100,000
VAT   20,000
Total   420,000

Fixed Assets
Land and buildings   200,000
Machinery   50,000
Total   250,000

Current Assets
Stock   70,000
Debtors   80,000
Cash in hand   20,000
Total   420,000

GEARING

The degree of gearing on a company impacts the shareholders prospect in the following ways.

Gearing is a term that refers to the capital structure of a company with respect to how much it has borrowed, and pays a fixed interest on to shareholders' funds. The company is said to be highly geared when it has high borrowings to shareholders' funds. A highly geared firm offers less potential to shareholders as there will be less available to share with them in the form of dividends after the interest has been paid. As a secondary effect the risk is increased as debt has to be serviced whereas shareholders are not guaranteed a dividend.

The level of gearing will have an impact on shareholders' willingness to invest. Some investors like to gear up their investment when bank interest rates are low and profit potential is high, other where cash flow will be tight may not want to see any debt and minimise fixed costs.

The benefit of being a director is that you can see monthly accounts and should have plenty of time to ensure that shareholders are presented with accounts that show the company in the best light possible, given the trading performance.

INVESTOR EVALUATION OF YOUR STOCK

How investors value your company's stock will depend on a number of factors and will not solely be based on rational thinking. It is best described as a half-objective-rational and half-subjective-inspirational process. The company's past performance can be no guarantee of its future performance but many chartists rely on trends to predict and, hence, value the share. In the "dot com" bubble, and to some extent still today, some firms are valued on their aspirations not their current profitability. The last significant factor in share price is the mood of the market. If it is pessimistic, prices fall; if it is optimistic, prices rise. The optimists are referred to as *bulls* and the pessimists *bears*. In a bull market, share prices rise; while in a bear market, prices fall. The market can make money in both conditions by buying and holding in a bull market until the price rises, and selling short in a bear market then repurchasing the stock at a later date when the price has fallen. Thus both situations can generate profits for the speculators and dealers.

Eventually profits will be what counts and until they are earned the share price may be more speculative than real. This can provide a company with a golden opportunity or be a poison chalice.

In the US pink slip market – a very risky place to raise capital – brokers often sell many more shares than the company offers in the hope that the company's share price will crash and they can buy back their paper at a much lower price than they sold it at.

Other market devices, such as spread betting, remove from the speculators the need to hold the stock and allow them to trade on margin a multiplier of the money they have to invest. This is highly risky and can result in huge gains or catastrophic losses. I suspect as many as 80% of those who play in this market lose money.

Share price fluctuations have an immediate impact on the company's valuation which, in turn, impacts on its ability to borrow and finance acquisitions, etc. It can also make the company vulnerable to a takeover bid. While there are share protection strategies available to reduce unwelcome takeover activity, the share price is critical for defending, or submitting to, such an attack.

Given the irrational factors, it is quite possible to use public relations tools to "spin" the company's position and impact the irrational or mood part of the company's share value, and in the short term this can support share prices at a higher level than they would otherwise be. But in the end it is hard profit that will be the critical factor that guarantees a solid share price.

Standard measures used to review a shares performance

There are four basic ratios that some investors use to judge a shares performance. These ratios should be monitored within the company as they can trigger investors to take action when they are not favourable or when they appear to undervalue your shares.

Dividend rate

The dividend rate is simply the amount of dividend divided by the nominal value of each share. If the nominal value of the share is £1.00 and the dividend is 20p, then the dividend rate is 20%.

Dividend yield

The dividend yield is calculated in the same way as the dividend rate, only substituting the nominal value of the share with the current share price. If a company's shares are trading for £2.00 and it declares a dividend of 20p, then the dividend yield is 10%.

Earnings yield

The dividend yield has limitations in determining the performance of the company because it only considers the dividend distributed. The amount of dividend is controlled by the recommendation of the board, and even when a company's profits are falling it may choose to increase or keep constant the dividend. In which case the dividend yield would remain the same or even improve. The earnings yield divides the net profits of the company by the market price of the share. So if, in year 1, a company generated £20,000 profit and had issued 100,000 shares with a year 1 price of £1.00, the earnings yield would be 20p/£1.00 = 20%. If, in year 2 the profits had fallen to £10,000, even though it still issued the same dividend and thus maintained the same dividend yield, the earnings yield would have fallen to 10%, assuming that the share price had not changed.

Price/earnings ratio

The price/earnings ratio (P/E ratio) is the market value of the share divided by the net profit per share. Thus, if the share price was £1.00 and net profit per share was 20p, the P/E ratio would be 5. This means that it would take the company five years to reach its full market value.

SUMMARY

- Company value is only half dependent on performance. There are other less rational factors at play.
- Past performance is no indication of future performance and can provide a less than adequate picture of the company's future.
- The published audited accounts are a snapshot of the company at a specific point in time. That point in time may not reflect accurately what the future holds.
- Irrational and mood factors play a significant part in share prices.

CHAPTER 12

FLOTATION AND BEYOND

If the stock market experts were so expert they would be buying stock, not selling advice.

Norman Augustine

It is the dream of many to see their company floated on the stock exchange. It can be highly rewarding but don't underestimate the risk and effort involved. There are several advantages to a flotation namely:

- A lower cost of capital
- Personal wealth
- Competitive position
- Prestige
- Benefit from market price fluctuations
- Increased ability to grow by acquisition

- Increased borrowing power
- Raise equity
- Employee attraction and retention
- Liquidity
- Valuation
- Succession planning.

Where there are advantages there are usually some disadvantages and flotation is no different. The disadvantages are:

- Expense
- Pressure to grow value
- Disclosure of information
- Red tape
- Loss of control
- Exposure to shareholder litigation
- Increased running costs
- Potentially paying more tax.

TO FLOAT OR NOT TO FLOAT?

The board needs to make the fundamental decision on whether or not the benefits outweigh the disadvantages. The results of this debate are merely the first and often last step in a journey towards flotation. If the board feel it is a good idea to float then they have to convince the shareholders of its merit. When the directors and the majority of shareholders agree – often required 75% in favour – the process can begin. The steps are:

1. The board feel it is beneficial to seek a listing.
2. Consultants provide a report on the benefits for shareholders to consider.
3. Shareholders consider the question and make a decision.
4. Appointment of advisory team.
5. Determination of optimum market conditions for flotation and likely window of opportunity is defined.

6. Plan is prepared.
7. Management team strengthened to fit institutional investor vision.
8. Share option plans initiated under inland revenue rules.
9. Grow the business on a "demonstrate worth" basis rather than "tax avoidance" basis.
10. Show steady sales and profit growth year on year.
11. Appoint non-executive directors and other advisory team members.
12. Determine investor acceptable founder exit strategies if appropriate.
13. Ensure clean audits and comply with governance standards.
14. Monitor the environment for optimal opportunity to float.
15. Selecting the underwriter.
16. Valuation.
17. Creating the prospectus.
18. Beauty parades.
19. Due diligence.
20. Registration.
21. Media relations.
22. Pricing.
23. Final prospectus.
24. IPO (Initial Public Offering).

As you can see, flotation is quite involved and can be viewed as a three- to five-year process.

The role of marketing in a flotation

Marketing plays a vital role in several of the above steps:

* The preparation of the overall IPO plan.
* The marketing balance on the management team.
* Generating the steady revenue growth and profitability.

- Ensuring that the right marketing advisers are appointed.
- Creating the prospectus.
- Beauty parade presentation materials and message.
- Media relations.

The preparation of the overall IPO plan

The process of flotation may take several years and therefore a detailed plan is essential. A famine to feast sales-cycle will not instil investor confidence, so a clear understanding of what is an invest-worthy company profile needs to be established early on, and the growth managed to meet the criteria.

You will recall the quote from the previous chapter about fashion, and this should be high on your mind. Making the company fashionable will allow you to gloss over the odd crack in the sales and revenue track record.

Like all plans, the environment will play a role in the timing of your IPO. Ideally you want to float during an up-cycle not at a crest because any delays will not play to your advantage. It is sometimes very difficult to judge the very best time to float and many IPOs have had to be cancelled at the last minute because of factors quite out of the control of the company, such as a stock market crash.

Naturally, the market intelligence derived from the marketing function would be the key that determines the optimum time for flotation. The choice of market can also play a role in the length of time required to achieve a successful IPO. There are basically two markets in the UK: AIM and The London Stock Exchange. AIM has less rigorous requirements in terms of:

- Company size
- Track record

- Number of shares in public hands
- Market capitalisation
- Admissions process.

For more information on AIM and the London Stock Exchange visit:

www.londonstockexchange.com

Consideration should also be given to designing the share structure in such a way as to make unwelcome takeovers less likely to succeed.

Detailed plans need to be prepared but care must be taken to ensure that the distraction of preparing for the flotation does not relegate to second place the fundamental business of marketing to paying customers. Design extra staff into the process and ensure that you are aware of your environment. Many firms have found that the distraction of flotation has meant that business has suffered and, as a consequence, the true value of the organisation was not realised on flotation.

The flotation plan must be integrated with the businesses marketing plan and the aims of both aligned to ensure they are both realised.

The marketing balance on the management team

While it is normal for financial specialist to lead the management team through the IPO process, it is also important that the marketing balance is maintained as, in my view at least, it is good marketing that makes the difference and is capable of turning an average flotation into a spectacularly successful promotion. Easyjet was a classic example in which the accounts at the time did not support a long history of profitability, but the style of the launch made it very successful.

Generating the steady revenue growth and profitability

Marketing is all about generating profitable sales by applying the full spectrum of marketing techniques and philosophies. The work becomes even more important in the lead up to an IPO. Any falter, PR gaffe or pricing error can mean the postponement or even cancellation of the IPO.

This should be the bread and butter to a successful marketing department, but the workload will have increased and profile-building activities not directed at bringing in customers will detract if they have not been budgeted for in the IPO plan. Most firm forget that marketing costs money, and if marketing is going to support a successful IPO it needs dedicated resources, not a dilution of its core-marketing budget.

Ensuring that the right marketing advisers are appointed

Many accountants and lawyers, as well as a host of other consultants, will be involved in the IPO process and it is also a good idea to hire experienced marketing assistance. My advice is to hire them in early at the profile building stage before the prospectus is prepared, and in that way they can reduce the IPO marketing spend by preparing the ground. They can also hold your hand through the period prior to filing, where any offer would be unlawful. When and what can be released must be carefully managed in accordance with the law. Consultants who have been through the process a few times can keep you right on all these matters.

It is a good idea to consider the changes that will need to be made to general marketing and promotional communications as a result of becoming a listed company. Any marketing communications that could be considered to influence the share price may land you in a lot of trouble with the regulatory authorities. This impacts on internal as well as external communications as allegations of insider trading abound when staff know more and sooner than shareholders of good or bad news.

Creating the prospectus

The prospectus is in effect the sales document despite all the caveats at the front, so clearly marketing input should be welcomed. The prospective process is iterative and the final prospects may be quite different from the original. Care must be taken to ensure that a balanced view of the company's position is documented and that any risks are clearly stated. (Quite likely stating these in a brochure will be a new idea to you if you are in any sector other than financial services, where it is an art form in itself.)

Beauty parade presentation materials and message

Having prepared the prospectus, the important task of convincing investors to part with their cash begins. This, like any sales presentation, requires excellent marketing support in the form of materials and well-trained and rehearsed presenters. If you have ever watched the television programme the "Lion's Den", where a panel of successful entrepreneurs invest their own money in new businesses, then you will have an idea of what these pitches can be like. They require the presentation team to be switched on, ooze experience and have a firm grasp of the business numbers.

Media relations

The gatekeeper and influencers also need to buy into your story as well as the financial press. In fact the whole spectrum of marketing communications needs to to be utilised to make an IPO successful.

As in all media relations, trying to build relationships and sell stories is not easy. Your IPO plan should have allowed you ample time to build contacts in the media and identify the key influencers and their media. I am surprised by how many IPOs try to gain a favourable story in too short a time frame. The important media should, by the time of the prospective launch, have followed your firm's evolution and hold favourable impressions about the company.

SUMMARY

- The building of a successful IPO is heavily dependent on the marketing and sales director.
- You, as marketing director, will be most responsible for achieving the sales growth that will ultimately lead to a successful IPO.
- The challenges are formidable but the rewards for all the hard work can be large.
- To successfully see an IPO through will guarantee you a place on the board of other hopeful IPOs and you will be in demand as a consultant and adviser.

CHAPTER 13

SHAREHOLDER VALUE

A cynic is a man who knows the price of everything and the value of nothing.

Oscar Wilde

The buzz word of any investor is "shareholder value" and it is key to retaining your executive post and for ensuring the prosperity of the company. Companies today do not necessarily have to make profits to have growing value; they don't even have to have sales but what they need to have is increasing shareholder valuations.

We have discussed the need to keep the investor informed and on side, but there are factors that play on the shareholders' minds and even completely unrelated events can change their perception of the firm's value, sending the shares tumbling or soaring for no reason connected with the governance of the company.

When a Scottish company cloned the world's first sheep, Dolly, and the then US president, Bill Clinton, asked for an immediate review of the implications, an American entrepreneur went out and recruited some of the best names in the industry in the USA and sold them on to a VC company for a huge profit. No strategy, no business plan, no money, just the feeling that these people would be worth the $1 million he had promised each of them if they joined him. Even before the scientists had served their notice in their old jobs he was a rich man and shareholders flocked to the new company to buy into "something big". "Carpe Diem" (seize the day) should be your motto when opportunities fall at your feet.

Why was it that this entrepreneur saw the opportunity yet others did not? The company that did the cloning raised a paltry sum in comparison to the entrepreneur and they had done the research, cloned the sheep, and had a business plan. Situational awareness is the key. When you can see the implications of events, there is opportunity for those brave enough, fast enough and perhaps naive enough not to understand the real risk involved.

Within the constraints of a corporate structure and account-ability, it is often difficult to grasp opportunities and by the time you have negotiated the bureaucracy the opportunity has long gone. It is necessary to have access to opportunity resources pre-assigned and available if windfall opportunities are to be grasped and shareholders' value expanded.

In one company, in which I have an involvement, the mecha-nism for raising finance was critical to the success or failure of the vision. The company is involved in the acquisition of property development sites and, as such, has to do a degree of due diligence on the sites it is considering acquiring. The value of the purchases runs into the tens of millions of pounds and investors want, have grown to expect, and will not tolerate less than good capital growth and return on investment in the UK property market. The traditional method of working in this market is to take each project to a group of investors and hope they will back the project. This all takes time, and each group of investors tends to like different types of projects and will be concerned about differing aspects of the site. This usually requires more work and delay in answering their specific questions before agreement to invest is reached. Then there is always the chance that they find themselves over committed and turn down a potentially valuable project for no other reason than they have no cash at that specific point in time. (For some reason they do not tell you this before you have wasted your time presenting to them.)

Speed is the essence and deals would take longer to agree and often slip into other hands because of the delays in agreeing a deal caused by investors' need, which is quite justified, to undertake due diligence and satisfy their specific likes and dislikes.

By structuring an offshore fund with different cells representing each project it was possible to raise a substantial sum of money at a reasonable rate of return. More importantly, it was not subject to the criteria of different investment model decisions. It could be accessed speedily and thus gave the company the ability to move faster, consider more property investment and make more money, more consistently and more assuredly than the traditional model was able to provide.

The key to marketing success is very often not in the traditional areas of site marketing or purchasing alone, but in designing mechanisms that increase shareholder as well as stakeholder value. The marketing challenge was not only to convince investors to accept less direct involvement in each purchase but also to convince them that, while on some projects their investment was perhaps not maximized, they would overall make more money than in cherry picking only the best, as most competitors could also see that and inevitably the price would be pushed up. By being able to make more deals in shorter time frames, the net result is a much more profitable operation that makes good margins on all investments and hence, due to the overall volume of business, makes more money more quickly.

Convincing shareholders to change their method of investing was a major challenge but one which, in the end, has paid off for everyone involved. Not all the original project investors made the change, but others made up the difference and are enjoying the rewards.

RETURN ON INVESTMENT

While working as a marketing manager you will most likely have been asked to justify your marketing expenditure. Perhaps you replied: "I know that half of our advertising is wasted, I just don't know which half." In reality marketing effectiveness is very crudely measured and many reports state that about 30% is not measured at all. This represents potentially very poor shareholder value for marketing expenditure. It is little wonder investors are reluctant to back marketing campaigns. Yet it is the marketing that creates the opportunity for sales to be made.

Considerable emphasis in your role as a marketing director must be placed on determining the Return on Investment (RoI) on the marketing expenditure. The board will support most RoI projects that show great value and marketing is not exempt from measurement in this regard.

In the pharmaceutical industry conferences have been organised on the topic. The third Annual Pharma Marketing Excellence Congress had as its strap line: "Create marketing excellence – implement powerful strategies that forecast, deliver and maximise RoI." Not a bad goal for a new marketing director?

Dividing the marketing activities of a typical company we can see there is a number of areas where marketing performance will directly impact not just marketing RoI but the business's RoI, and therefore these will be the areas to concentrate upon.

However before considering the RoI in the key areas of:

• Market research
• Communications

- Sales
- Customer satisfaction

we need to consider a definition of "marketing productivity." While there has been a lot of work in this area and several definitions have been suggested, for example,

- Barger (1955), goods distributed per man-hour;
- Sevin (1965), sales per marketing expense or profit per marketing expense;
- Drucker (1985), units of output per employee; number of successful new products per time period, or number of staff members;
- Michaluk (2000), GMAS model;

marketing productivity is in essence the maximisation of marketing's effectiveness and efficiency. You might also say it is about doing the right things in marketing in precisely the right way. In order to achieve this laudable goal it is necessary to have real-time/right-time feedback so that action can be taken to ensure that levels of efficiency are maintained and that, as the market changes, the right things are getting done to ensure your continued marketing success.

RoI adds a third financial dimension to effectiveness and efficiency. Sevin (1965) defines marketing productivity as "the sales or profit output per unit of marketing effort". An insightful notion, but very difficult to measure. The problem is that there is often a time delay in marketing effort returning sales volume, market share or profits making it difficult to attribute marketing effort to sales results, while there are a number of other factors outside the control of marketing that can rob a company of profits or market share, such as strikes and unforeseen bad debts. I do not think many suppliers thought that Enron, Red Letter Days, and numerous other well-respected names would fail, owing them money.

To avoid the problem of profit measurement many have turned to "profit-ability" measurement, distinguishing profit from profit-ability based upon time. "Profit-ability" is a promise of future profits while "profit" is historically determined and is usually real. Using my own 3F model I define "profit-ability" as a factor of Faith, while profit should in most cases be "Fact". Whether "profit-ability" turns out to be Fact or Fiction is determined by the passage of time and the accountant's pen. (I think it would have been a lot less confusing if they had simply adopted the term "profit-potential".)

Utilising profit-ability analysis, a kind of optimist's "profit-ability and loss-ability" statement can be generated. This statement varies very little from a traditional profit and loss statement other than by the fact that it includes attributable marketing and sales costs – for example, sales management, advertising, promotion, sales force expenses, market research, customer satisfaction measurement. Using "profit-ability" a RoI of sorts can be calculated.

Some of the best business minds have turned their attention to the tricky problem of calculation RoI in marketing activities: Paul Goodman, Tom Peters, Peter Drucker, to name but a few. Drucker introduced such concepts as multi-criterion measures and suggested utilising moving averages to smooth profit-ability. Then the Boston Consultancy group introduced the familiar BCG matrix, and the Profit Impact of Market Strategies (PIMS) was born from the analysis of 3,000 business units in 450 companies. From these models came predictive models and all sorts of claims such as Buzzell and Gale (1970) and Gale's *Harvard Business Review* article, where they claimed a 10% increase in share of market accounts for a 5% increase in RoI. This model has been heavily criticised over the years and even more elaborate models have been introduced, such as Mehrotra's "Brand Franchise" model where loyalty of customers is factored into sales generated and Gross's "Ratio Approach" where a set of ratios has been proposed.

A valuable summary of all these methods was created by Bonoma and Clark (1988) in *Marketing Performance Assessment* (see Table 13.1) and the mediating factors are shown in Table 13.2.

Tables 13.1 and 13.2 are very useful, because if you choose any of the former performance measures and like the results, they are a "true measure", and if you don't like the results, you can always use the latter mitigating factors to dismiss the results, on single or multiple factor grounds. You can't lose!

There is currently no single reliable way of measuring marketing success in every situation. You will have to choose the best fit you can for your particular market, products or services, and compare your performance with a "matched spectrum" company to truly know the efficiency and effectiveness of your marketing. Many of the mitigating factors listed above are poor excuses and your marketing intelligence system should have warned you of their impact well before they hit your sales figures.

The one over-lying truth is that you have to measure something and you have to be aware of the implications of that measurement. The old saying "what gets measured gets done" has to be tempered with "what gets measured gets counted as done".

Table 13.1 Performance assessment factors

Marketing expenses	Investment	Number of employees
Man–hours	Quality of employees	Quality of decisions
Number of transactions	Square feet	Technology
Administrative overhead	Effort	Profit
Sales income	Sales volume	Market share
Cash flow	Intermediate activities	Stock turnover
Innovation	Service	Quality of service
Value added	Customer franchise	

Table 13.2 Mediating factors for performance assessment

Supplier industry structure	Channel structure	Competition
Market volatility	Market size changes	Timing of market entry
Per capita consumption of product category	Inflation	Product proliferation
Market practices	Technology change	Life-cycle position
Product differentiation	Product cost structure	Product mix
Cost of servicing	Customer growth	Customer mix
Brand loyalty	Magnitude and frequency of activities	Ability to monitor task performance
Transaction size	Transaction frequency	Company or employee capability
Economies of scale	Vertical Integration	

The NHS waiting times fiasco is a classic example. A simple change of definition of what constituted being on a waiting list gave the impression that waiting time had been reduced while patients were finding no change in the time they had to wait for treatment.

Ensure that your measurement is a real indicator of performance, and be especially sure that it is a leading indicator. Finally, have something to compare it with. I remember leasing a small Robinson R22 helicopter out at £95 per hour, having been "reliably" informed that the going rate was £85 and thinking I had done well, only to discover that many leasing companies were charging £105 per hour. That margin in a year equated to lost sales income and direct additional profit of £4,800. A failure to ensure reliable market intelligence before setting the price had saved me a few hours' work and cost me £4,800 per annum for the life of the contract (3 years = £14,400). I know I get paid well but not that well for a few hours' work and a competent researcher would have cost only around £70 for 2 hours' work. A RoI of a massive 20,571%.

The cost of marketing failures can be significant and you must ensure that when you are measuring performance you are adhering to the best practice within your industry.

THE OLD MILITARY MODEL OF SELECTION

I cannot remember where the matrix shown as Table 13.3 came from, but I would like to apologise to any members of the armed forces in advance for its light-hearted view of their very necessary and dangerous profession.

You can see from the matrix that hard-working intelligent individuals become officers. Stupid and hard-working individuals join the cavalry – after all there is a lot of work involved in looking after horses. Those unfortunates who are judged to be both stupid and lazy – and up in the infantry (cannon fodder), while those lazy intelligent individuals are assigned to administration on the grounds that they will find the easiest and fastest way to do things to enable them to relax more.

Expectation

In measuring marketing performance two factors need to be understood: management's perceptions of effort and management's performance expectations.

Table 13.3 Candidate matrix

	Intelligent	*Stupid*
Hard working	Officers	Cavalry
Lazy	Administration	Infantry

I am sure the intelligent and lazy administrators would be clever enough to give the perception of exceptional effort being involved in the tasks they had simplified and streamlined, while the perception of the infantry soldier would be that of the box in which they find themselves (lazy and stupid). How we manage these groups and therefore measure their performance will very much depend on our perception, and it is therefore essential to have an accurate perception of reality. I would suspect that if we were setting targets for the groups in the matrix we would have high outcome expectations from the officers and low output expectations from the infantry.

From Figure 13.1 you can see that expectations play a major view in determining how we perceive results. It is important that we take time and effort in setting our expectations to ensure that they encompass a wide view of all aspects of the business as our expectations will impact our actions and results achieved.

So, like most things in business, knowing the people and their characteristics plays a vital role in setting expectations and in reliably understanding whether the strategy is at fault or the

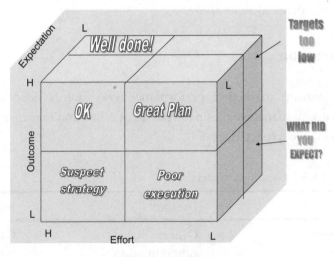

Figure 13.1   Expectations–outcomes–effort cube

implementation is being poorly executed. The STORM model discussed in earlier chapters is key to effective evaluation of RoI and ensuring that correct action is being implemented even when you have initially misjudged the effort, or have erroneous expectations (type 1 and type 2 errors).

SUMMARY

To achieve an accurate measurement of marketing and delivery of a good RoI, we need to consider the following questions:

1. Can we define a specific marketing programme as a divisible entity from the overall marketing effort?
2. Can we attribute all the actions, effort and costs to the programme accurately?
3. Has what constitutes success been defined and, if so, has it been stated in a SMART (Specific, Measurable, Achievable, Realistic and Time-framed) form?
4. Have the results of the programme been compared to the SMART expectations?
5. What are the costs per unit of success measurement?
6. Can we determine if others, in a similar environment, or from our own historic records, have obtained better or worse results in the past?
7. Are there any "real" mitigating factors?
8. Has the marketing spend been worth the rewards?
9. Can we learn to do things better in future?

If you are able to answer "yes" to all the questions above, then you will be well on the way to achieving an improved RoI on your marketing effort. Placing this within the context of a SMART model will ensure you of an improving situation regardless of the accuracy of your start point.

CHAPTER 14

COMPETENCE, INTEGRITY, HONOUR AND TRUST

Virtue is its own punishment.

Aneurin Bevan

THE DIRECTOR'S ROLE

The role of the board has been discussed in Chapter 1 but the role of any director is governed by the company's Memorandum and Articles of Association as well as general company law. The details of company law change from time to time but can be found in the current Companies Act 2006. It is a good idea to have a working knowledge of the various companies acts in the countries in which you work.

In general they prevent you from making a personal profit from your "insider knowledge"; they stipulate the extent of your powers; you are expected to act in good faith and in the interest of the company; you will have a duty of care; you will need shareholders' approval for some decisions, e.g. giving yourself a golden handshake or parachute, and service contracts above five years.

Some people, however, take a different view.

I know more than a few managers who are running very large successful companies, and who have lurched from one disaster to another throughout their careers yet always somehow managed to survive – always coming out of each company they destroy smelling of roses. As Jeffrey Archer the novelist, fundraiser, former chairman of the Conservative Party, Member of the House of Lords, and former convict showed, you can rise very high before the past catches up with you.

In business, some failures have been very highly rewarded, e.g. Procter & Gamble former CEO Durk Jager got $9.5 million after a mere 9 months at the head of P&G with stock down 50%, costing P&G shareholders some $70 million, while *Business Week* estimates that Mattel Inc. have to sell 600,000 Barbie dolls each year to pay the $1.2 million annual pension of their former CEO Jill Bared as part of her $50 million severance package. *Business Week* also supplied a list of severance packages paid to former CEOs: Bank One, $10.3 million; Coca-Cola, $25.5 million; Walt Disney, $38.8 million; and Conesco, $49.3 million. In the UK Railtrack had been severely criticised for similar payoffs to its executives at a time when the company was experiencing major problems and was finally wound up by the government.

So clearly a good lawyer and a good director's contract with a golden parachute is the order of the day. However, I think these large payoffs are becoming a thing of the past as shareholders demand a lot more transparency in appointments and remuneration systems in the companies in which they invest, and are generally less inclined to pay for poor performance. However, there are still some companies that are so desperate for a leader that they may offer you almost any terms. After all, if a past-his-best footballer can get $1 million a week, how much is the head of a major corporation with significant brand value worth?

Some companies are bigger than some countries and have considerable economic and political power. One British company under investigation for bribery managed to have the investigation halted by a Prime Minister on the grounds of "national security". In many countries, despite the damage to their countries' wealth, bribery and corruption are almost endemic. The technical term, I am told, for handling bribery and corruption is "local business practices" and it is normal to have a local company handle that for you and pay them a service fee. Several very large names in the corporate world have had to explain rather embarrassingly exactly what some local agents do for their money.

Thankfully, like huge pay for poor performance, these areas of dubious business ethics are gradually, though shareholder pressure, being reduced or at least better camouflaged.

The world is unfortunately full of rogues and they come in all colours and sexes, so *caveat emptor*.

The rewards must come in heaven for whistle-blowers as they certainly do not appear here on earth. Most become unemployable and penniless. If you see wrong, therefore, it is better to follow the golden rule of: "See no evil, hear no evil, and speak no evil, but get out of there fast."

When you assume the role of marketing director, ensure that the people around you exhibit the same levels of integrity, honour, respect and decency that you do. Above all, ensure that you can trust them, otherwise move on to greener pastures.

Being honest, truthful and trustworthy are not the three most likely attributes to bring you great wealth, but they do make it easier to sleep at night and you will never fear more than the average citizen from a knock on the door from the police.

I trust you have a successful and rewarding career as a marketing director and that you overcome every challenge and have fun, because it is one of the most exciting things to be, on any board.

Good luck!

MARKETING MANAGEMENT SERVICES INTERNATIONAL LTD.

Annual General Meeting

26th January 2007

AGENDA & NOTES

Agenda item	Minutes	Actions arising
Apologies for absence		
Minutes of previous meeting		
Business arising from minutes		
Correspondence		
To receive the directors' statement		
To receive the Accounts for the financial year 2005/6		
To reappoint the auditors		
To elect/re-elect directors		
Any Other Business (AOB)		
Date of next meeting		

GRANT THORNTON
RESEARCH

Risk Management Services
Fifth FTSE 350 **Corporate Governance Review 2006**
Highlighting trends in compliance

Grant Thornton 🜚

Contents

Part of the Grant Thornton **thinking** series

1

Introduction

Welcome to our fifth annual review of corporate governance disclosure by the FTSE 350. Three hundred and fourteen companies have been assessed against the terms of the Combined Code 2003 (the Code) and associated guidance in order to profile disclosure practices and trends. This year we have refreshed our approach by directly comparing individual companies' disclosures this year to last, in order to gauge whether they are truly updating and enhancing their explanatory narratives or merely rolling them forward, "boilerplate", year-on-year.

Overview

Our review confirms a continuing improvement in governance disclosure but also throws out a challenge to all UK plc directors to embrace the true spirit of the Code by resisting the temptation to merely repeat disclosures given in the previous years and furthermore to the non-executive directors to champion compliance by challenging any proposed departures as to whether they are truly in the interests of their stakeholders.

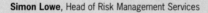

Simon Lowe, Head of Risk Management Services

2

Foreword

Landscape – UK
During the 12 months since our last review the corporate governance landscape has continued to evolve in the UK, throughout Europe and the rest of the world. In the UK, Douglas Flint's review focused on refreshing the Turnbull guidance on internal control, we saw some fine tuning of the Code as a result of a refresh exercise by the Financial Reporting Council (FRC) and there were a number of amendments to the Companies Act, notably the consideration around the Operating and Financial Review (OFR).

Landscape – Europe
In Europe, the fourth, seventh and eighth Directives are gradually being incorporated into corporate life. The Directives now formalise the need for companies to issue an annual corporate governance statement, to indicate whether or not they have complied with a code of governance, to formalise the need for disclosing information about the companies' control and risk management systems and to appoint an audit committee. In the UK, existing or draft legislation already reflects these, and directors will be very aware of the influence the Directives are having, for example in terms of their heightened responsibility to disclose all relevant information to the auditors.

This growing level of awareness and importance now being placed on corporate governance by a wide range of stakeholders is confirmed by the 2006 ISS Global Institutional Investor Study in which it was found that 78% of European institutional investors surveyed believe corporate governance will become "significantly or somewhat more important over the next three years" in Europe.

Message from America
In the US, there has been a growing clamour to apply a more risk-based approach to SOX partly driven by inflated implementation costs (particularly Section 404), but also due to growing concern at the flight of registrants away from the US exchanges. Conservative interpretation of the requirements of Section 404 and the available guidance, have driven additional cost into compliance regimes of many companies. This has, albeit somewhat belatedly, now been recognised by the regulators.

The US Securities and Exchange Commission (SEC) is currently looking to reduce the costs of assessing and auditing internal control, while still achieving the intended benefits. To that end, both the Public Company Accounting Oversight Board (PCAOB) and the SEC are devising revised guidelines to assist management and auditors in this regard.

A draft amended version of Auditing Standard 2 (AS2) for auditors and further guidance for companies to determine how to conduct an effective evaluation of internal controls, are due to be issued in December. However, if these fail to adequately address the issue of cost, it is highly likely that Congress will have to intervene to implement some level of exemption from Section 404. US vice president Dick Cheney, speaking recently about SOX, hinted at such a possibility. The imminent retirement of Senators Paul Sarbanes and Michael Oxley will perhaps provide the catalyst for change.

Scepticism abounds
Europe remains to be convinced as to the softening of SOX and its impact on European governance. The reaction of the UK government to NASDAQ's possible interest in the London Stock Exchange and the European reaction to NYSE's interest in Euronext confirms that scepticism abounds. In both instances the regulatory authorities are seeking to establish a right of veto (in one form or another) over any US corporate legislation crossing the Atlantic.

3

UK considerations
Concern re US legislative creep

Should UK directors be worried about the threat of legislative creep, or is it inevitable that the market will, over time, harmonise around a common, global approach to governance practice? After all, stakeholders want the same thing – consistent, reliable, honest, comparable accounting and reporting, coupled with low investment costs and easy access to capital.

Sight should not be lost of the governance principles the US Congress were seeking to embed into corporate practice through the introduction of SOX legislation, as they are not so dissimilar to Europe's. The US's reaction to corporate mismanagement is increasingly being seen as having given rise to something of an over reaction amongst those responsible for implementing it. Over time it seems inevitable that pressure, not least from those with vested interests in the capital markets, will lead to a more pragmatic approach to the application of the legislation.

The risk for UK plc is that it becomes complacent, choosing minimum disclosure rather than truly demonstrating its commitment to the principles to the Code, as such an approach could open the door to more prescriptive regulation.

Findings

Our 2006 review raises some interesting challenges for public company boards. It confirms the continued progress that has been made by the UK's larger plcs in complying with the Code.

However, looking more closely at those areas which allow for judgment and discretion as opposed to a straight yes or no, the picture is slightly different as the trend suggests a tailing off in those companies voluntarily giving additional, informative disclosure. For example, in the area of risk and internal controls, only 38 companies, a figure very similar to the previous year, have chosen to go the extra mile with their explanations. Furthermore, our review identified that only 31 companies provided enough disclosure to be considered fully compliant with the Code (see question 1), leaving some 90% falling short of full compliance. It is true that the majority of these companies provide explanations for their non-compliance, but this raises the question of whether companies are hiding behind the "comply or explain" option.

Spotlight on compliance

Common perception suggests that "comply or explain" are equal options. Whilst the Listing Rules do give the option, the emphasis of the Code is very much on compliance. With a large majority of companies feeling they can justify departure from the Code, perhaps choosing "departure" has become simply too easy.

The challenge

This year's review highlights both the improving trends and high standards of governance now practised by UK plc. But it also throws down a challenge to those charged with governance to truly embrace the spirit of the Code and so ensure the future of our principles based approach. Ultimately it is the degree to which UK plc chooses to apply the Code principles which will determine the future of our governance practices.

4

Executive summary

Taking time to "comply"?

Companies still need further time to adapt to the revisions made to the Code back in 2003.

With only 34% of the FTSE 350 claiming full compliance (an increase from 28% last year), the trend suggests that two more years will be required before the number of companies claiming full compliance reaches previous levels observed under the original version of the Code (54% of the FTSE 100 and 42% of the Mid 250 considered themselves fully compliant in our 2003 review).

But does "full compliance" really mean full? Our review could only identify 10% of FTSE 350 companies whose disclosure fully supported this claim. This either casts doubt on the rigour applied to the self-assessment of compliance, or suggests that key disclosure requirements have been omitted from their narratives. Companies should resist the temptation to simply "roll forward" their corporate governance statement and instead revisit the Code (in particular Schedule C), which lists out the specific disclosure requirements.

Comply or explain – a matter of convenience or better for the stakeholder?

Whilst specific reference is made to "comply or explain" in the Listing Rules, it is the Preamble, not the body of the Code, which refers to this option. And it is not a simple either/or, rather the emphasis is on "complying...most of the time" and departing only if it can be justified with considered explanations.

Given this emphasis it is surprising to find 66% of companies still choosing to depart from the Code's provisions, in one regard or another.

Considered explanation or boilerplate

In this year's review, we have seen further improvement in the degree to which companies are providing reasoning for areas of non-compliance, with 96% providing at least some explanation, up from 91% last year. However this disguises the true picture. This year we assessed whether companies actually update their disclosure year-on-year. Our aim was to draw out the prevalence of the so-called "boilerplate" disclosures which undermine the comply or explain approach. Of those companies who provide explanations of non-compliance, only 32% have made any significant change since the previous year and 57% made no change at all.

Key areas of improvement

Last year, the improvement story was audit committees. This year, it is board accountability, as evidenced by the strengthening of disclosures in respect of the authority and role of the non-executive directors. For example, 28% more companies are providing greater detail on the work of the nomination committee, including the processes it uses to evaluate appointments to the board. Encouragingly, the largest increase comes from the Mid 250 where a third more companies made this disclosure.

Nearly 20% more companies (70% overall) now provide a statement that the non-executive directors conduct an annual performance appraisal on the chairman. This is supplemented by additional 6% of companies (now 89% overall) who provide at least some description of how the board, committees and individual directors are evaluated. Whilst this represents a marked improvement, the residual question and a current "hot topic" (although not possible to assess from disclosure alone), is the effectiveness or otherwise of these evaluations. Anecdotally, there is a consensus amongst chairmen and non-executive directors, that best practice has yet to emerge.

Interestingly, 24% more companies now make the terms and conditions of the appointment of non-executives available, but despite this improvement, this remains one of the most frequent areas of non-compliance.

5

Pushing full compliance

Almost full marks are now being achieved in the following areas:

- identification of key role holders on the boards and committees (99%)
- a statement of how the board operates (97%)
- disclosure of the number of meetings and attendance during the year (99%)
- disclosure of the steps taken to understand the views of shareholders (98%).

The cynic might suggest that the majority of improvements are either "quick wins" or "boilerplate" enabled as they don't change year-on-year and no improvement in physical governance practice is required. However, this may be unfair as perhaps one of the greatest recent successes has been Sir Robert Smith's work in raising the audit committee's prominence, with 97% of companies now providing a separate report on the role and processes of that committee.

Directing the business – independence and accountability

For 23 of the companies reviewed, the chairman and chief executive are the same individual, and two-fifths of these were in the same position last year. For the small number of companies where the chief executive has become the chairman during the year under review, while the Code discourages this, around 80% disclosed that this was specifically discussed with shareholders, as required under the revised Code. Some further progress has been made in balancing the board with an appropriate independent non-executive element – 70%, up from 64% last year, all driven by increases in the Mid 250. However, that still leaves 94 companies with a majority of executive directors.

Role of the committees

In regard to the composition of committees, 88% of audit, 86% of remuneration and 92% of nomination committees are now in line with the Code, compared to 77%, 68% and 92% respectively last year.

Further progress has been made to ensure that the audit committee contains at least one member with recent and relevant financial experience. The FTSE 100 lead the way with 86% compliance, with the Mid 250 catching up, at 76%. Whilst there is no requirement to state who the individual is, it is encouraging to see the majority of these companies now being prepared to identify this key person.

6

Internal control reporting – the old...

Ninety eight percent of companies continue to provide a statement that a review of the effectiveness of the group's internal controls has been undertaken, and 82% now provide some form of summary as to how this assessment has been made. This is a significant increase from around two-thirds of companies last year. Progress was made by both the FTSE 100 and the Mid 250 in this respect. Within this statement, 85% of companies now explicitly state that their review covers a range of controls of an operational and compliance nature as well as financial – the highest level of disclosure during the five years of this review.

Conversely, this is also the area which continues to be one of the most challenging areas for compliance, as the principle requires companies to apply judgment as to the application of the Code, rather than giving a straight yes or no. An indication of such challenge is the fact that only a small number of companies, 38 (22 FTSE 100 and 16 Mid 250 companies), achieve what we consider to be "outstanding" levels of disclosure.

...and the new

We also looked for signs of early adoption of Douglas Flint's revisions. One of the key changes proposed by his review was the need for disclosure that necessary action has been (or is being) taken to remedy any significant failings or weaknesses identified in their systems of internal control.

Contrary to the US, the true incidence of significant weaknesses is difficult to ascertain, as companies are not explicit in admitting whether any significant weaknesses were actually identified. This may in part explain the low figures, as less than 20% of the FTSE 350 made appropriate disclosures, and the majority of these referred to the existence of a process rather than a specific event.

The business review and disclosing risks

The Chancellor withdrew the requirement for the OFR and with it the requirement to disclose principal business risks, in late 2005. However, amendments to the Companies Act relating to the "business review", introduced to comply with European Directives, are now in force for companies with years ending after 31 March 2006. These require similar disclosures to the OFR, particularly in the respect of key business risk.

Annual reports within our review would not, in the main, have been required to apply the new "business review" protocols. However, the vast majority of companies, 80%, made valiant attempts to accord with the principles.

But whilst there is continued improvement in disclosures relating to the process of identifying risks, a sizeable percentage of companies, 23% of the FTSE 100 and 53% of the Mid 250, still do not give an indication as to what their principal business risks are.

7

Internal audit

A key element to any company's assurance framework is the operation of an internal audit function. But around 3% of the FTSE 100 and 20% of the Mid 250 still have no internal audit function, be it internal, or outsourced. Of those with such a function, only 45 companies went as far as disclosing who, whether internal or external, provided that assurance. While 80% of companies have stated that the audit committee "monitor and review the effectiveness" of internal audit activities, only around 14% appear to have initiated an external effectiveness review.

Corporate responsibility

Relatively large numbers of companies disclose the existence of processes dedicated to social responsibility reporting. They provide at least an overview of activities in the body of the annual report, and outline policies on responsible behaviour relating to their interaction with key stakeholders. Some improvement was noted in the provision of quantified results against corporate responsibility objectives, but a gulf remains between the FTSE 100 with 81% (2005 - 79%) and the Mid 250, 40% (2005 - 34%).

Independent verification of these results may become an increasing area of focus with corporate responsibility reporting moving from nice to do to having a hard commercial impact. The government is already indicating that as part of its procurement procedures demonstrable social responsibility performance is set to become a prequalification hurdle. So there is still a considerable amount of work to be done, as only 5% of the Mid 250 and 13% of the FTSE 100 were able to state that their activities had been independently verified.

Conclusion

As governance practice continues to evolve around the world, the review identifies a number of welcome improvements but also picks up on a note of complacency, which the UK plc directors should ignore at their peril.

8

Corporate governance – general

Question 1: Do they claim full compliance with the Combined Code?
Guidance: "The following additional items must be included in its annual report and accounts: ...a statement as to whether the listed company has complied throughout the accounting period with all relevant provisions set out in Section 1 of the Combined Code." (Listing Rule 9.8.6(6)(a))

Figure 1 (%)

FTSE 350
34.1
27.6
57.8
45.8
36.1

FTSE 100
42.9
41.0
62.6
54.1
41.4

Mid 250
30.1
21.5
55.6
41.8
31.7

2006
2005
2004
2003
2002

The main message:

Companies appear to still be taking time to adapt to the revisions made to the Combined Code in 2003. The most common areas of non-compliance disclosed were A.4.4 (terms and conditions of appointment of non-executive directors), C.2.1 (internal control effectiveness) and C.3.1 (audit committee independence and financial experience).

Whilst a third of the FTSE 350 did claim full compliance, only around 10% of the FTSE 350 reviewed (31 companies) appeared to have made all of the disclosures that are expected by the Code to support this claim. Whilst companies simply may not be making disclosures on all relevant governance practices that they have in place, this does raise questions over what "full" compliance really means.

9

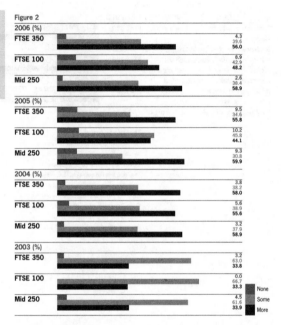

Question 2: If not compliant, to what degree do they explain their reason for non-compliance?
Guidance: "A company that has not complied with the Code must include in its annual report and accounts a statement setting out the company's reasons for non-compliance." (Listing Rule 9.8.6(6)(b)(iii))

Figure 2

2006 (%)

FTSE 350	4.3 / 39.6 / **56.0**
FTSE 100	8.9 / 42.9 / **48.2**
Mid 250	2.6 / 38.4 / **58.9**

2005 (%)

FTSE 350	9.5 / 34.6 / **55.8**
FTSE 100	10.2 / 45.8 / **44.1**
Mid 250	9.3 / 30.8 / **59.9**

2004 (%)

FTSE 350	3.8 / 38.2 / **58.0**
FTSE 100	5.6 / 38.9 / **55.6**
Mid 250	3.2 / 37.9 / **58.9**

2003 (%)

FTSE 350	3.2 / 63.0 / **33.8**
FTSE 100	0.0 / 66.7 / **33.3**
Mid 250	4.5 / 61.6 / **33.9**

None
Some
More

The main message:

There has been an overall improvement in the level of explanation given by companies who do not fully comply with the Combined Code. Now 96% of companies (previously 90%) provide at least some explanation as to the reasons for non-compliance.

10

Non-executive directors

Question 3: Is at least half of the board comprised of independent non-executive directors?

Guidance: "Except for smaller companies, at least half the board, excluding the chairman, should comprise non-executive directors determined by the board to be independent." (Combined Code, A.3.2)

Figure 3 (%)

FTSE 350
69.7
64.0
62.5

FTSE 100
79.6
80.0
74.7

Mid 250
65.3
56.6
56.9

■ 2006
■ 2005
■ 2004

The main message:

A steady increase for the Mid 250 where nearly two-thirds now have a balance of independent directors on the board. The FTSE 100 has remained at around the same level as last year, but of the FTSE 100 that were also not compliant last year, half have failed to address the balance since.

Question 4: How well do companies describe the consideration of independence?

Guidance: "The board should identify in the annual report each non-executive director it considers to be independent." (Combined Code, A.3.1)

The main message:

An improvement in the level of detail for the FTSE 100, with the Mid 250 being consistent with last year. Whilst 20 companies still do not disclose any information to describe how they consider their non-executive directors as independent, if at all, one in ten companies demonstrated a noticeable improvement in the level of explanation given year-on-year.

Example: The qualification for board membership includes a requirement that all our non-executive directors be free from any relationship with the executive management of the company that could materially interfere with the exercise of their independent judgement. In the board's view, all our non-executive directors fulfil this requirement. All have received overwhelming endorsement at successive AGMs, at which they are now subject to annual election. The integrity and independence of character of these directors are beyond doubt.

Figure 4

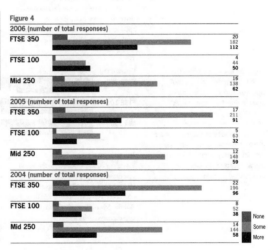

2006 (number of total responses)

FTSE 350
20
182
112

FTSE 100
4
44
50

Mid 250
16
138
62

2005 (number of total responses)

FTSE 350
17
211
91

FTSE 100
5
63
32

Mid 250
12
148
59

2004 (number of total responses)

FTSE 350
22
196
96

FTSE 100
8
52
38

Mid 250
14
144
58

■ None
■ Some
■ More

Question 5: Is it disclosed that the terms and conditions of appointment of non-executive directors are available for inspection?

Guidance: "The terms and conditions of appointment of non-executive directors should be made available for inspection." (Combined Code, A.4.4)

Figure 5 (%)

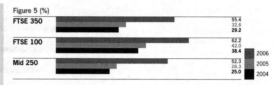

FTSE 350
55.4
32.6
29.2

FTSE 100
62.2
42.0
38.4

Mid 250
52.3
28.3
25.0

2006
2005
2004

The main message:

Whilst companies appear to have taken heed to what was highlighted in last year's review, (reflected in the big improvements in disclosure levels particularly in the Mid 250), this is still one of the weakest areas of compliance. 55% of companies now disclose that their terms and conditions of appointment of non-executive directors are available for inspection. In many cases the terms and conditions appear to exist, but it was not disclosed that they are available for inspection. This simple disclosure will bring them in line with the Code. Whilst there is clear progress year-on-year, three years have passed and there is still some way to go. Even the FTSE 100 appear to have taken their time with this one.

Question 6: Led by the senior independent director, do the non-executive directors meet without the chairman at least annually to appraise the chairman's performance?

Guidance: "Led by the senior independent director, the non-executive directors should meet without the chairman present at least annually to appraise the chairman's performance." (Combined Code, A.1.3)

Figure 6 (%)

FTSE 350
70.1
52.4
35.9

FTSE 100
75.5
61.0
43.4

Mid 250
67.6
48.4
32.4

2006
2005
2004

The main message:

Strong growth in compliance for the second year running by both the FTSE 100 and Mid 250. However, 30% of companies overall still make no specific statement that the chairman's performance is appraised by the non-executives on an annual basis. This demonstrates the learning curve experienced in this area. The standard is set by a handful of companies that disclose a greater level of detail of the processes used, including performance questionnaires, formal performance appraisal processes, and consultation with executive directors and major shareholders.

12

Board and committees – general

Figure 7

2006 (%)

FTSE 350
2.9
49.4
47.8

FTSE 100
0.0
29.6
70.4

Mid 250
4.2
58.3
37.5

2005 (%)

FTSE 350
4.7
59.2
36.1

FTSE 100
1.0
49.0
50.0

Mid 250
6.4
63.9
29.7

None
Some
More

The main message:

A strong increase in disclosure levels this year, particularly for the FTSE 100. Nearly half of all companies are now providing "more" than the bare minimum disclosure.

Example: To discharge its governance function in the most effective manner...the board has laid down rules for its own activities in a governance process policy. The process policy covers:

- the conduct of members at meetings
- the cycle of board activities and the setting of agendas
- the provision of timely information to the board
- board officers and their roles
- board committees – their tasks and composition
- qualifications for board membership and the process of the nomination committee
- the evaluation and assessment of board performance
- the remuneration of non-executive directors
- the process for directors to obtain independent advice
- the appointment and role of the company secretary.

13

Question 8: Does the report identify the chairman, chief executive, senior independent, members and chairs of the nomination, audit and remuneration committees?
Guidance: "The annual report should identify the chairman, the deputy chairman (where there is one), the chief executive, the senior independent director and the chairmen and members of the nomination, audit and remuneration committees." (Combined Code, A.1.2)

Figure 8 (%)

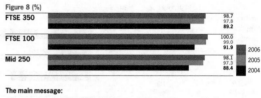

The main message:
All companies in the FTSE 100 clearly identify all the key members of their boards and committees. The Mid 250 are not far behind, and have moved further towards full compliance.

Question 9: Is the number of meetings of the board and overall attendance disclosed?
Guidance: "[The board] should also set out the number of meetings of the board and those committees and individual attendance by directors." (Combined Code, A.1.2)

Figure 9 (%)

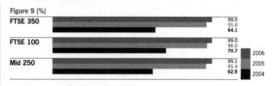

The main message:
Further steady improvements have been made this year. Companies appear not to have struggled to implement this additional disclosure requirement introduced in 2003 and less than 1% of all companies in the FTSE 350 fail to provide this information.

14

Question 10: Are the roles of the chairman and chief executive divided and exercised by different individuals?
Guidance: "There should be a clear division of responsibilities at the head of the company between the running of the board and the executive responsibility for the running of the company's business." (Combined Code, A.2)

Figure 10 (%)

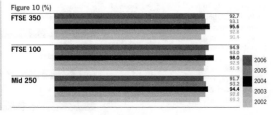

	2006	2005	2004	2003	2002
FTSE 350	92.7	93.1	95.6	92.8	90.4
FTSE 100	94.9	93.0	98.0	92.9	91.9
Mid 250	91.7	93.2	94.4	92.8	89.2

The main message:
The slight overall drop in compliance can be attributed to the new members of the FTSE 350, whilst a small improvement has been observed in the FTSE 100. Of the 23 companies that were non-compliant last year however, 10 companies still have not split these roles. This suggests that companies are either finding it hard to attract the right candidate, or the chairman believes in the old adage "If I'm not broke don't fix me !"

Question 11: For new chairmen that were appointed during the year...
a) if they previously held the role of CEO, has his/her independence been assessed and fully disclosed?
Guidance: "A chief executive should not go on to be chairman of the same company." (Combined Code, A.2.2)
b) if the chairman also chairs another FTSE 100 company, has there been consultation on the level of commitment needed and relevant disclosure made?
Guidance: "No individual should be appointed to a second chairmanship of a FTSE 100 company." (Combined Code, A.4.3)

Figure 11a (%)

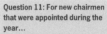

	%	
FTSE 350	80.0	
FTSE 100	66.7	
Mid 250	85.7	2006

The main message:
Ten companies have appointed the CEO to chairman during the period subject to our review. Eight of these fully disclosed this fact.

Figure 11b (%)

	%	
FTSE 350	33.3	
FTSE 100	33.3	
Mid 250	N/A	2006

The main message:
Three FTSE 100 companies have a newly appointed chairman that chairs another FTSE 100 company. Only one company fully disclosed that they considered the time commitments required prior to appointment.

Question 12: How much explanation is there of how the board, committees and individual directors are annually evaluated formally for their performance?
Guidance: "The board should state in the annual report how performance evaluation of the board, its committees and its individual directors has been conducted." (Combined Code A.6.1)

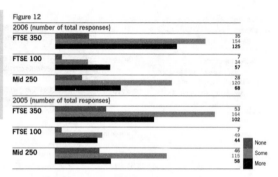

Figure 12

2006 (number of total responses)

FTSE 350 — 35 / 154 / 125

FTSE 100 — 7 / 34 / 57

Mid 250 — 28 / 120 / 68

2005 (number of total responses)

FTSE 350 — 53 / 164 / 102

FTSE 100 — 7 / 49 / 44

Mid 250 — 46 / 115 / 58

■ None
■ Some
■ More

The main message:
There has been an overall reduction in the number of companies who gave no disclosure at all on performance evaluation, and a greater number of companies (now 40% from 31% last year) provided "more" than minimal levels of explanation.

One in five companies appeared to have updated their disclosure from last year and 14% of companies showed improvement in the quality of disclosure provided.

Question 13: Is it disclosed that the terms of reference for the audit, remuneration and nomination committees is available for inspection?
Guidance: "The terms of reference of the audit committee, including its role and the authority delegated to it by the board, should be made available." (Combined Code, C.3.3)
"The remuneration committee should make available its terms of reference, explaining its role and the authority delegated to it by the board." (Combined Code, B.2.1)
"The nomination committee should make available its terms of reference, explaining its role and the authority delegated to it by the board." (Combined Code, A.4.1)

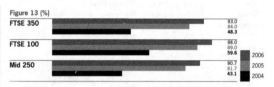

Figure 13 (%)

FTSE 350 — 93.0 / 84.0 / 48.3

FTSE 100 — 98.0 / 89.0 / 59.6

Mid 250 — 90.7 / 81.7 / 43.1

■ 2006
■ 2005
■ 2004

The main message:
Further steps have been made towards full compliance with good improvements made in both the FTSE 100 and Mid 250 disclosure and the majority of companies made reference to the availability of this information on their

website. As with question 5, the terms of reference may be available, but still some companies fail to provide this simple disclosure.

16

Audit committee

Question 14: Are all the members independent non-executive directors?

Guidance: "The board should establish an audit committee of at least three... members, who should all be independent non-executive directors."
(Combined Code, C.3.1)

Figure 14 (%)

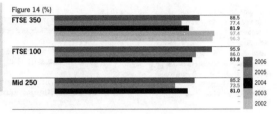

FTSE 350
88.5
77.4
81.9
97.4
96.3

FTSE 100
95.9
86.0
83.8

Mid 250
85.2
73.5
81.0

- 2006
- 2005
- 2004
- 2003
- 2002

The main message:

This year witnesses strong improvement across the FTSE 350, indicating further evidence that the authority and influence of the audit committee continues to grow. Surprisingly, four of the FTSE 100 and 32 of the Mid 250 still don't comply.

Question 15: Do they have an internal audit function or equivalent?

Figure 15 (%)

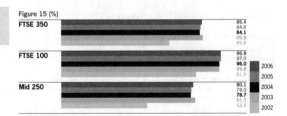

FTSE 350
85.4
84.6
84.1
85.9
65.8

FTSE 100
96.9
97.0
96.0
95.9
81.8

Mid 250
80.1
79.0
78.7
81.3
52.5

- 2006
- 2005
- 2004
- 2003
- 2002

The main message:

The number of companies in the FTSE 350 that have an internal audit function has remained steady for the third year running. Internal audit departments continue to be much more prevalent in the FTSE 100 than the Mid 250 and of those companies that have such a function, 45 disclosed that they have at least a partially if not fully outsourced service to a third party. Of those companies that were non-compliant last year, a massive 88% still have not implemented such a function.

17

Question 16: Does the audit committee monitor and review the effectiveness of internal audit activities?
Guidance: "The main role and responsibilities of the audit committee should … include … to monitor and review the effectiveness of the company's internal audit function." (Combined Code, C.3.2)

Figure 16 (%)

FTSE 350	79.0 / 81.8 / 69.1 / 69.9 / 65.6
FTSE 100	90.8 / 90.6 / 72.6 / 95.9 / 81.8
Mid 250	73.6 / 76.8 / 67.1 / 61.3 / 52.5

2006 / 2005 / 2004 / 2003 / 2002

The main message:
Progress has stagnated this year in both the FTSE 100 and Mid 250. The Mid 250 are still lagging behind the FTSE 100, perhaps due to a lack of resources to implement such a thorough effectiveness review (see also question 17 below).

Question 17: If the committee performs such a monitoring function, is there specific reference to an internal audit effectiveness review?
Guidance: "The main role and responsibilities of the audit committee… should include; to monitor and review the effectiveness of the company's internal audit function." (Combined Code C.3.2)
"Internal assessments should include: Ongoing reviews of the performance of the internal audit activity; and periodic reviews performed through self-assessment or by other persons within the organisation." (International Standards for the Professional Practice of Internal Auditing – 1311)
"External assessments should be conducted at least once every five years. The potential need for more frequent external assessments as well as the qualifications and independence of the external reviewer or review team, should be discussed with the board. Such discussions should also consider the size, complexity and industry of the organisation." (International Standards for the Professional Practice of Internal Auditing – 1312)

Figure 17 (%)

FTSE 350	14.3
FTSE 100	19.4
Mid 250	12.0

2006

The main message:
C.3.2 of the Code recommends that there should be an ongoing effectiveness review of the internal audit department, guidance brought in by the Smith report. This is further supported by the International Standards from the Institute of Internal Auditors, who state that at least every five years this assessment should be conducted by an external party.

The percentage of companies that disclose that a specific internal audit effectiveness review has been carried out during the year may appear low at first glance, but on average we perhaps might only expect one in five companies to have had an external review this year.

18

Question 18: If there is currently no internal audit function, is the absence of the function explained and is there disclosure that a review of the need for one has been carried out during the year and a recommendation been made to the board?
Guidance: "Where there is no internal audit function, the audit committee should consider annually whether there is a need for an internal audit function and make a recommendation to the board, and the reasons for the absence of such a function should be explained in the relevant section of the annual report."
(Combined Code, C.3.5)

Figure 18 (%)

The main message:
Of the companies in the FTSE 350 that don't have an internal audit function, 43 out of 46 are in the Mid 250. However, the vast majority of these companies (41) do at least provide an explanation as to why such a function has not been created, and that the board has reviewed the need for such a function during the year.

Question 19: If the auditor provides non-audit services, is there a statement as to how the auditor's objectivity and independence is safeguarded?
Guidance: "The annual report should explain to shareholders how, if the auditor provides non-audit services, auditor objectivity and independence is safeguarded." (Combined Code, C.3.7)

Figure 19 (%)

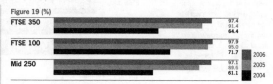

The main message:
Both the FTSE 100 and Mid 250 are embracing the Code guidelines in respect of non-audit services being provided by the auditor, with nearly all companies now providing a statement of how auditor objectivity and independence has been safeguarded. The Mid 250 have now caught up with the FTSE 100. This would further indicate the increasing seriousness with which companies are taking the Code's guidelines on transparency and accountability for audit activities, despite a lack of mandate such as Sarbanes-Oxley.
    Most companies also provide a brief statement on the policies or systems employed to ensure auditor objectivity and independence is not compromised.

19

Question 20: Does the audit committee state it has at least one member with recent and relevant financial experience?
Guidance: "The board should satisfy itself that at least one member of the audit committee has recent and relevant financial experience." (Combined Code, C.3.1)

Figure 20 (%)

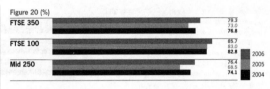

FTSE 350 — 79.3 / 73.0 / 76.8
FTSE 100 — 85.7 / 83.0 / 82.8
Mid 250 — 76.4 / 68.5 / 74.1

2006
2005
2004

The main message:

The FTSE 350 as a whole has seen positive movements in assigning this specific responsibility. The majority of companies reviewed not only make the statement but explicitly identify the member of the committee deemed to have the "recent and relevant experience". This is perhaps refreshing in this increasingly litigious age. However, 65 companies either fail to formally identify such an individual, or their audit committees appear to lack the requisite experience.

Question 21: Is there a separate section of the annual report which describes the work of the committee?
Guidance: "A separate section of the annual report should describe the work of the committee in discharging those responsibilities." (Combined Code, C.3.3)

Figure 21 (%)

FTSE 350 — 97.1 / 93.1 / 81.0
FTSE 100 — 98.0 / 95.0 / 87.9
Mid 250 — 96.8 / 92.2 / 77.8

2006
2005
2004

The main message:

A year-on-year improvement by both the FTSE 100 and the Mid 250 demonstrates the continual raising of profile of the audit committee, as the descriptions of the work of the audit committee are becoming more transparent and accessible to readers of the accounts. Some companies that do not comply did describe the committee's remit, but not within a separate section as required by the Code. However, only one in five companies reviewed have improved the quality of disclosure from last year.

20

Remuneration committee

Question 22: Are there at least three members, all of whom are independent non-executive directors?

Guidance: "The board should establish a remuneration committee of at least three, ...members, who should all be independent non-executive directors."
(Combined Code, B.2.1)

Figure 22 (%)

	2006	2005	2004
FTSE 350	85.7	67.7	84.8
FTSE 100	92.9	79.0	86.9
Mid 250	82.4	62.6	83.8

The main message:

There is a significant increase in compliance levels this year, particularly in the Mid 250. This is mainly due to a large number of companies who have appeared to have recruited to the committee (and/or replaced a member with) an independent non-executive in accordance with the Code, which is consistent with the increase in board balance (see question 14).

Question 23: If the chairman does sit on the committee, does he/she chair it?

Figure 23 – 2006 FTSE 350 (number of total responses)

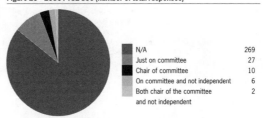

N/A	269
Just on committee	27
Chair of committee	10
On committee and not independent	6
Both chair of the committee and not independent	2

Figure 23 – 2006 FTSE 100 (number of total responses)

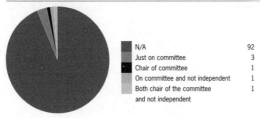

N/A	92
Just on committee	3
Chair of committee	1
On committee and not independent	1
Both chair of the committee and not independent	1

21

Question 23: If the chairman does sit on the committee, does he/she chair it?

Figure 23 – 2006 Mid 250 (number of total responses)

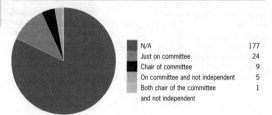

N/A	177
Just on committee	24
Chair of committee	9
On committee and not independent	5
Both chair of the committee and not independent	1

The main message:

The revised Code proposes that the chair of the board may only be a member of the remuneration committee if he or she was considered independent on appointment, and should not chair the committee.

There are a number of companies, of whom the vast majority are in the Mid 250, that do not comply with this revised guidance. Whilst these changes to the Code were not expected to be applicable to any of the companies in this year's review, it is interesting to note the existing position on a much debated area.

It seems at first glance that the extent of the issue and the resultant change in the Code is not supported, however, many companies may have improved their governance prior to the subsequent relaxation. This will be interesting to monitor again next year.

22

Question 24: Does the company state the potential maximum remuneration available including performance related elements?
Guidance: "The performance-related elements of remuneration should form a significant proportion of the total remuneration package of executive directors..." (Combined Code, B.1.1)

Figure 24 (%)

The main message:
Approximately 15% of the FTSE 350 do not disclose an upper limit on the potential maximum remuneration for directors. This may be attributable to companies having a "variable bonus pool" from which to draw performance related elements, depending on the level of the firm's success in the year.

Question 25: Is it stated that the board (or shareholders where required) sets the remuneration for the non-executive directors?
Guidance: "The board itself or, where required by the Articles of Association, the shareholders should determine the remuneration of the non-executive directors." (Combined Code, B.2.3)

Figure 25 (%)

The main message:
A decrease in relevant disclosure in the Mid 250 has led to a drop in the overall compliance from last year. A higher proportion of new entrants to the FTSE 350 are in the Mid 250 rather than the FTSE 100 and these companies may not yet have adapted to the guidance on performance related pay and corresponding disclosure.

23

Nomination committee

Question 26: Are the majority of members non-executive directors and is the chairman either chairman of the board or a non-executive director?
Guidance: "A majority of members of the nomination committee should be independent non-executive directors. The chairman or an independent non-executive director should chair the committee." (Combined Code, A.4.1)

Figure 26 (%)

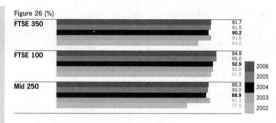

The main message:

A similar level of compliance to last year. Many chairmen sit as the chair of the nomination committee, showing a keenness to remain influential in the selection of board members.

Question 27: Is there a description of the work of the nomination committee, including the process it has used in relation to board appointments?
Guidance: "A separate section of the annual report should describe the work of the nomination committee, including the process it has used in relation to board appointments." (Combined Code, A.4.6)

Figure 27 (%)

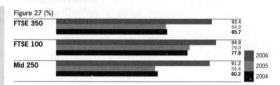

The main message:

There has been a large increase in the number of companies who are becoming compliant in this area of the Code, particularly in the Mid 250. The inclusion of details of the appointment process, as well as ensuring there is a separate section for the nomination committee within the report has helped to increase the compliance levels in this area.

In years where there have been no appointments to the board, companies tend to omit a statement confirming that there is a formal procedure in place for when appointments are made.

The amount of detail given in the description of the work of the nomination committee is higher for FTSE 100 than Mid 250. Around a third of the Mid 250 give the bare minimum amount of detail, whilst a quarter of all the FTSE 350 set the standard by providing more. The gap between the levels of compliance in the two groups has closed considerably in the year.

24

Turnbull compliance – internal control and risk management – revised Combined Code

Question 28: Is there a statement that a review of the effectiveness of the group's internal controls has been undertaken at least annually?
Guidance: "The board should, at least annually, conduct a review of the effectiveness of the group's system of internal control and should report to shareholders that they have done so." (Combined Code, C.2.1)

Figure 28 (%)

FTSE 350   98.4 / 99.4 / 93.7 / 82.0
FTSE 100   100.0 / 100.0 / 96.0 / 90.8
Mid 250   97.7 / 99.1 / 92.6 / 77.9

2006
2005
2004
2003

The main message:
Although the disclosure level is still close to full compliance, overall there has been a slight drop from last year, which again can be attributed to the turnover of companies entering the FTSE 350 this year.

Question 29: Is there a statement that this review covers all material controls including financial, operational and compliance controls and risk management systems?
Guidance: "The review [of the effectiveness of the group's system of internal control] should cover all controls, including financial, operational and compliance controls and risk management." (Combined Code, C.2.1)

Figure 29 (%)

FTSE 350   84.7 / 79.9 / 74.9 / 69.6 / 40.2
FTSE 100   90.8 / 83.0 / 79.8 / 71.4 / 39.4
Mid 250   81.9 / 78.5 / 72.7 / 68.8 / 40.8

2006
2005
2004
2003
2002

The main message:
The number of companies that state that the review of the effectiveness of the internal controls includes all types of controls, has increased in this year's review. A steady increase in compliance year-on-year suggests that companies are demonstrating greater acknowledgment of the consideration of other control types during internal control reviews, beyond purely financial. Companies therefore appear to be getting the message, but there is still some way to go, suggesting a need for further education, particularly for the Mid 250, or simply better disclosure on existing processes.

25

Question 30: Is there a statement that there is an ongoing process for identifying, evaluating and managing the significant risks faced by the company?

Guidance: "In its narrative statement of how the company has applied Code principal D.2 [C.2.1 in the revised Code], the board should, as a minimum, disclose that there is an ongoing process for identifying, evaluating and managing the significant risks faced by the company, that it has been in place for the year under review and up to the date of the approval of the annual report and account."
(Turnbull, paragraph 35)

Figure 30 (%)

	2006	2005	2004	2003
FTSE 350	98.1	94.7	88.9	81.0
FTSE 100	99.0	96.0	91.9	83.7
Mid 250	97.7	94.1	87.5	79.8

The main message:

The principle of this question is that the internal controls of a company should evolve and be kept continuously under review to adapt to the changing nature of risks. The results of this year's review suggest that the vast majority of companies have fully adopted the Turnbull principles in this respect.

Question 31: Do they give an indication of what their principal business risks are?

Figure 31 (%)

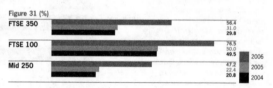

	2006	2005	2004
FTSE 350	56.4	31.0	29.8
FTSE 100	76.5	50.0	49.5
Mid 250	47.2	22.4	20.8

The main message:

The number of companies that give an indication of their principal business risks has increased further this year. Despite the OFR requirements being dropped, there is still a requirement for this disclosure under amendments to the Companies Act, although these would have only applied to a minority of companies in this year's sample (those with year-ends on or after 31 March 06). The Mid 250 appear to be more sensitive to the potential impact on competitive advantage that this disclosure may have.

Question 32: Is there an apparent consideration of risks relating to other key stakeholder matters?

Figure 32 (%)

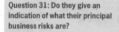

	2006	2005
FTSE 350	44.9	44.9
FTSE 100	59.2	56.0
Mid 250	38.4	38.4

The main message:

The consideration of other key stakeholder matters within the identified business risks has remained at the same level as last year. It is the FTSE 100 who continue to lead the way.

26

Question 33: Is there information to assist the understanding of the company's main features of its risk management and internal control process?

Guidance: "The board may wish to provide additional information in the annual report and accounts to assist understanding of the company's risk management processes and system of internal control." (Turnbull, paragraph 36)

Figure 33

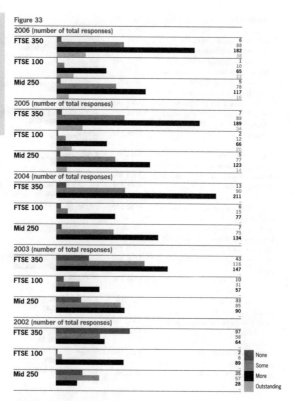

2006 (number of total responses)

FTSE 350		
	6	
	88	
	182	
	38	

FTSE 100
1
10
65
22

Mid 250
5
78
117
16

2005 (number of total responses)

FTSE 350
7
89
189
34

FTSE 100
2
12
66
20

Mid 250
5
77
123
14

2004 (number of total responses)

FTSE 350
13
90
211

FTSE 100
6
15
77

Mid 250
7
75
134

2003 (number of total responses)

FTSE 350
43
116
147

FTSE 100
10
31
57

Mid 250
33
85
90

2002 (number of total responses)

FTSE 350
97
58
64

FTSE 100
2
8
89

Mid 250
35
57
28

None
Some
More
Outstanding

The main message:

A marginal improvement in results from last year, with the standard still being set by just less than 40 companies that are deemed as "outstanding" for their level of useful additional information provided.

The main message:

We see a general improvement of the detail of disclosure from last year. Of particular note is the FTSE 100 where only one in ten companies have no summary of the review process, dropping from approximately a quarter last year.

Of the 30 companies that are new to our sample this year, 27 are new to the Mid 250. Three-quarters of these have given no detail of the review of effectiveness. This illustrates a possible need for better quality advice on following the Turnbull guidance to smaller cap companies, prior to entering the FTSE 350.

For the other companies in the Mid 250, it would appear that 32 companies have moved from giving no summary to providing some disclosure in this regard.

Overall however, the figures for the FTSE 350 who provide neither are still perhaps disappointing (18%) and only 27% appear to really "think Turnbull".

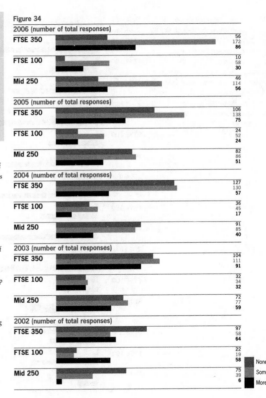

Figure 34

2006 (number of total responses)

	None	Some	More
FTSE 350	56	172	86
FTSE 100	10	58	30
Mid 250	46	114	56

2005 (number of total responses)

	None	Some	More
FTSE 350	106	138	75
FTSE 100	24	52	24
Mid 250	82	86	51

2004 (number of total responses)

	None	Some	More
FTSE 350	127	130	57
FTSE 100	36	45	17
Mid 250	91	85	40

2003 (number of total responses)

	None	Some	More
FTSE 350	104	111	91
FTSE 100	32	34	32
Mid 250	72	77	59

2002 (number of total responses)

	None	Some	More
FTSE 350	97	58	64
FTSE 100	22	19	58
Mid 250	75	39	6

None
Some
More

28

Question 35: Does the company disclose that any necessary actions have been or are being taken to remedy any significant failings or weaknesses?

Guidance: "In relation to Code provision C.2.1, the board should summarise the process it has applied in reviewing the effectiveness of the system of internal control and confirm that necessary actions have been or are being taken to remedy any significant failings or weaknesses identified from that review." (Revised Turnbull guidance, paragraph 36)

Figure 35 (%)

FTSE 350	18.8
FTSE 100	18.4
Mid 250	19.0

2006

The main message:

Companies may not be confident in disclosing negative comments and would prefer not to mention this in their reports. However, this goes against the nature of the "comply or explain" policy of which the Code and associated guidance relies upon to hold credibility with investors and other stakeholders. Companies that disclose weaknesses or areas of improvement give assurance that their effectiveness reviews are working well.

29

Shareholder relations

Figure 36 – 2006 (%)

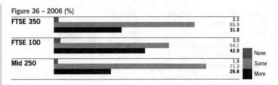

FTSE 350 — 2.2 / 65.9 / 31.8
FTSE 100 — 3.0 / 54.1 / 42.9
Mid 250 — 1.9 / 71.3 / 26.8

None
Some
More

The main message:

More than 97% of companies are providing at least some information in this area (last year 98%). On average the FTSE 100 gives more detail than the Mid 250, which perhaps again demonstrates the greater resources available for investor relations and the greater degree of consultation given by companies with larger market capitalisation.

Whilst companies are relatively good at communicating their views on the company to the shareholders, they are generally weaker at providing specific information on how the views of shareholders have been understood.

Example: The company has a programme of communication with its shareholders. As well as share price information, news releases and annual reports, the website includes speeches from the AGM, presentations to the investment community and a section for shareholder services. The board believes that the AGM presents an important opportunity for dialogue with private shareholders, many of whom are also our customers. Representatives from across the Group are available and all shareholders have the opportunity to cast their votes. Shareholders can register...the company.

30

Corporate responsibility

Question 37: Have they established dedicated structures and processes to direct and regularly monitor the company's wider social environment and ethical performance and report to the board?

Figure 37 (%)

FTSE 350	90.4 / 90.3 / 94.6 / 43.1
FTSE 100	99.0 / 99.0 / 99.0 / 58.0
Mid 250	86.6 / 86.3 / 92.1 / 36.1

2006 / 2005 / 2004 / 2003

The main message:

Nearly 100% of the FTSE 100 and 90% of all companies reviewed have some structure in place for the direction and monitoring of corporate responsibility matters, in keeping with previous years.

Question 38: Is the disclosure within the annual report?
Guidance: "The guidelines take the form of disclosures, which institutions would expect to see included in the annual report of listed companies." (Association of British Insurers (ABI) – Guidelines on Socially Responsible Investment, section 2)

Figure 38 (%)

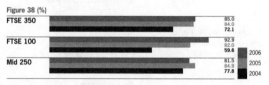

FTSE 350	85.0 / 84.0 / 72.1
FTSE 100	92.9 / 82.0 / 59.6
Mid 250	81.5 / 84.9 / 77.8

2006 / 2005 / 2004

The main message:

The FTSE 100 continue to approach full disclosure in this area, with an improvement of over 10% on last year. Many companies have separate corporate social responsibility reports available on their websites. Within the annual reports there are reduced versions, with references to the full reports. This has been considered acceptable disclosure.

In contrast, the Mid 250 companies have performed slightly worse in comparison with last year. This again could be explained by the level of company turnover on the index where new companies may take time to be able to report the wealth of information that many of the FTSE 350 currently provide.

Question 39: Is there a statement of company policy regarding issues such as energy/natural resource consumption, employment, recycling, carbon emissions etc?

Figure 39 (%)

FTSE 350	90.4 / 90.3 / 88.6
FTSE 100	99.0 / 100.0 / 94.9
Mid 250	86.6 / 85.8 / 85.6

2006 / 2005 / 2004

The main message:

FTSE 100 companies continue to give more detail of company policy, and targets for socially responsible actions.

31

Question 40: Are such policy objectives stated with quantified results?

Figure 40 (%)

	2006	2005	2004
FTSE 350	52.2	48.3	41.9
FTSE 100	80.6	79.0	66.7
Mid 250	39.4	34.3	30.6

The main message:

While the FTSE 100 results have remained consistent with the previous year, the Mid 250 has seen a slight increase in disclosure. Given that nearly 90% companies in the FTSE 350 have specific policies on corporate responsibility matters, it is disappointing that so many in the FTSE 350 fail to support these with some disclosure on quantified progress against policy objectives.

Question 41: Are disclosures verified by an independent (external) third party?

Figure 41 (%)

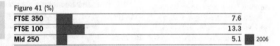

	2006
FTSE 350	7.6
FTSE 100	13.3
Mid 250	5.1

The main message:

Proportionally more FTSE 100 than Mid 250 companies are having their corporate responsibility disclosures independently reviewed. This figure may be set to rise as more industries follow the government's lead on pre-qualification based upon corporate responsibility factors.

32

The future of governance

Question 42: Does it appear that the company has provided a separate business review in the directors' report in accordance with Section 234ZZB of the Companies Act?

Figure 42 (%)

FTSE 350	79.3
FTSE 100	85.7
Mid 250	76.4

2006

The main message:
As the amendment to the Companies Act requires a business review, it would appear companies are pre-empting any potential penalties by drafting business reviews/OFRs within the annual report as a matter of priority.

Note:
For the first time, companies listed on the Hong Kong Stock Exchange are having to comply with a code of governance which largely mirrors the UK Code. Grant Thornton Hong Kong has reviewed the disclosure practices of some 200 major companies in the Hang Seng Composite Index (HSCI) and the published results provide for an interesting comparison between Hong Kong's performance and the mature practices of the UK (www.gthk.com.hk).

Grant Thornton Risk Management Services

For more information
To find out how Grant Thornton may be of assistance to you and your business, please contact:

London
Simon Lowe
Head of Risk Management Services
T 0870 991 2451
E simon.j.lowe@gtuk.com

Philip Keown
Partner – Risk Management Services
T 0870 991 2394
E philip.r.keown@gtuk.com

Martin Gardner
Partner – Risk Management Services
T 0870 991 2847
E martin.n.gardner@gtuk.com

Midlands
Eddie Best
Partner – Risk Management Services
T 0870 991 2849
E eddie.j.best@gtuk.com

North
Barrie Senior
Partner – Risk Management Services
T 0870 991 2135
E barrie.senior@gtuk.com

34

About Grant Thornton

We are the UK member of Grant Thornton International, one of the world's leading international organisations of independently owned and managed accounting and consulting firms. These firms provide a comprehensive range of business advisory services from around 520 offices in over 110 countries worldwide. Although Grant Thornton International is not a worldwide partnership, the firms share a commitment to providing the same high quality service to their clients wherever they do business.

For further information contact your nearest Grant Thornton office or visit our website at www.grant-thornton.co.uk

Belfast
T 028 9031 5500
Trevor Blayney

Birmingham
T 0121 212 4000
Steve Line

Brighton
T 0870 381 7001
Ellen Walsh

Bristol
T 0117 926 8901
Mark Aldridge

Bury St. Edmunds
T 01284 701271
Mike Burrows

Cambridge
T 01223 225600
John Corbishley

Cardiff
T 029 2023 5591
Louise Evans

Cheltenham
T 0845 026 1250
Mark Aldridge

Edinburgh
T 0131 229 9181
Robert Hannah

Farnham
T 01252 734 345
Robin Rowe

Gatwick
T 0870 381 7000
Ellen Walsh

Glasgow
T 0141 223 0000
Robert Hannah

Ipswich
T 01473 221491
James Brown

Kettering
T 01536 310000
Steve Robinson

Leeds
T 0113 245 5514
Andrew Moore

Leicester
T 0116 247 1234
Garry Meakin

Liverpool (Mersey)
T 0151 224 7200
Howard Hackney

London
T 020 7383 5100
Mark Henshaw

London Thames Valley
T 0870 733 6700
Jim Rogers

Manchester
T 0161 834 5414
Graeme Whittaker

Milton Keynes
T 01908 660666
Phil Barrett

Newcastle
T 0191 261 2631
Andrew Moore

Northampton
T 01604 623800
Steve Robinson

Norwich
T 01603 620481
James Brown

Nottingham
T 0115 948 3483
Garry Meakin

**Oxford
(Oxfordshire)**
T 01865 799899
Tracey James

Poole
T 01202 308000
Stephen Mills

Reading
T 0870 733 6700
Paul Etherington

Sheffield
T 0114 255 3371
Garry Meakin

Southampton City
T 02380 221 231
Stephen Mills

**Southampton
Segensworth**
T 01489 864200
Stephen Mills

This publication has been prepared only as a guide. No responsibility for loss occasioned to any person acting or refraining from acting as a result of any material in this publication can be accepted by us.

Grant Thornton

Grant Thornton
thinking

GLOSSARY OF MARKETING TERMS

Activity Based Costing (ABC)

ABC very basically, measures activity costs based on the process driver and the resources consumed. All activities have a purpose: inputs and outputs. ABC measures the activity and allocates costs to the outputs. It differs from traditional costing models in the level of detail and accuracy it provides. This detail and accuracy allows management to make process improvements to meet cost objectives and provides performance measures.

Arthur D. Little life-cycle matrix

This model builds on the product life-cycle model by adding another avenue of investigation − "competitive position". This is a rather intricate model because of the complex nature of life-cycle planning and competitive position. This model is best applied to companies whose market is fast changing because changes to product life cycles can have a weighty impact on them.

Balanced Scorecard (BSC)

BSC converts a company's operations and strategy into an inclusive list that supplies the structure for a tactical assessment and control system. BSC supplies an organisation with expertise, which it needs to guide potential triumph. It offers an organisation's corporate level personnel with a complete structure that interprets its operations and strategy into a logical set of performance indicators.

The financial view

The ultimate objective of this view is to "improve shareholder value". Improved shareholder value comes as a consequence of the offsetting of income growth against increased productivity within the company. The factors of income growth and productivity both consist of two main subsections. Within income growth, the contributing factors are the expansion of the market and the increasing of income from the present client base. The two factors that lead to increased productivity are increased efficiency and better use of current resources combined with large investments being replaced by gradual investments.

The customer view

This section has been described as "the heart of the strategy". This area outlines the exact strategy for gaining new custom or for enlarging the current customers' division of business.

The internal view

This view outlines the corporate processes and exact actions that company must perfect in order to maintain the customer view, which as has already been said is fundamental to the model.

Learning and growth view

This view outlines the "unquantifiable" resources that are necessary in order to allow the goals of organisational actions and client/company interaction to be carried out at increasingly sophisticated levels. There are three main sections to be considered within the learning and growth view. The first is that of strategic capabilities. This section encapsulates the knowledge and abilities demanded from the staff in order to maintain the strategy. The second section is that of "strategic technologies". This part is concerned with the technological requirements that are necessary to maintain the strategy. The third and final area that contributes to the learning and growth view is that of environment for activity. Within this part the effect of shifts in the social atmosphere of the organisation are taken into account as the optimum environment in which to maintain the strategy is examined.

Benchmarking

Benchmarking is the strategy of studying the competition's products, services, or practices to improve your own company or business.

Boston Consultancy Group Growth Share Matrix

This model presupposes that the quiescent cash flow of a particular product is proportional to the enlargement of the market as a whole in relation to its competitors and its present market share. One clear advantage of this model is its universal application, which allows parallels and contrasts to be drawn between widely differing products.

Critical assumptions

The "facts" on which the strategic plan is based. In order to make a decision, in the absence of perfect information, assumptions are made. If these assumptions turn out to be erroneous and these would have a substantial material impact on the organisation, then they are considered critical.

Citicorp interaction analysis

Because neither top-down nor bottom-up strategic planning models fully encapsulated Citicorp's style, they adopted a more complex matrix model.

The first step in their interaction analysis is to recognise important assets of each business unit and identify any overlap between these. Secondly, all major responsibilities of each business unit must be established and any overlap pinpointed. The third and final step in the analysis is to judge the level of interdependence that exists between the business units and to establish the strategic consequences of this.

Closed domain market

This is a market in which all prospective customers can be identified.

Customer Relationship Management (CRM)

CRM is a system that gives a complete overview of the client/company exchange. CRM involves itself in every means of communication and exchange between the organisation and the customer. A CRM programme is customised to effectively meet the needs of any individual organisation's customers' requirements.

Dow-corning strategy matrix

The Dow-corning model's starting point is placed in the hands of senior members of management who are obligated to formulate objectives. Because objectives can often straddle a number of borders (be they departmental or systematic), the manager who formulates the objective then goes on to navigate the objective's path through the company maze until it has reached its implementation point. This ensures that critical strategies are completed effectively.

Dynamic Insight

GMAS provides reporting systems using a system developed in-house called Dynamic Insight. This system allows research results to be delivered securely and dynamically, so that users can request whichever survey and the period the want to look at and have the results generated in real time. From the broadest results overview, respondents can drill down to find out who gave a particular response to a particular question, at a particular time. The purpose of Dynamic Insight is that it gives authorised users access to research being gathered in real-time at the right time in the right format for the users' purpose.

Enterprise Neuron Trail (ENT)

The critical internal communication channels within an organisation encompassing formal and informal means of exchange.

Enterprise Resource Planning (ERP)

The term "enterprise resource planning" was derived by the Gartner Group in the last decade of the twentieth century to relate company software applications. ERP involves the consolidation of all units and operations across an organisation into an individual computer application that can assist specific needs and enable contact within the organisation, as well the common use of data that is produced by the application.

Fuzzy logic

Enables imprecise approximations to be interpreted and reasoned in a manner that strongly resembles human thought processes. Fuzzy logic does not see information as merely "true" or "false", it can distinguish gradations of truthfulness to lead to a conclusion that indicates that something may be, for example, 70% true and 30% false.

General Electric matrix

This model follows a similar line as the Boston Consultancy Group (BCG) Growth Share Matrix. BCG's model used two main factors to measure the appeal of the market and the infallibility of the company. However, in contrast, the General Electric matrix employs a large number of determinants to measure these. The result of employing a large number of determinants is that General Electric's matrix is not as rigid as BCG's and can be adapted by varying the determinants to allow effective utilisation in the most unusual of sectors.

Harrigan–Porter end-game analysis

Harrigan and Porter developed this model that would provide a number of substitute tactics for companies placed in receding industries. In addition to this, the model can assist the organisation in establishing the most suitable strategy at that particular time. This model can help, in addition to companies in declining industries, those with products entering the last stage in their life cycle.

Irrefutable research

Research that is valid and free from bias is irrefutable. The concept can be summed up using the formula $M = R + B$. What we measure (M) is equal to the real answer (R) plus the bias (B). There is always bias of some kind or another, e.g. interviewer, question design, and sample. Irrefutable research aims to eliminate as much bias as possible, therefore reflecting better the true result.

King's strategic-issue analysis

This model allows managers and analysts to come to a point of broad agreement. In addition to this, the model facilitates the improvement of decision-making on issues and the incorporation of dissection of those issues within the normal planning system.

Local Area Network (LAN)

A computer network that is confined to a small area (such as a building or ship, for example). Although the LAN exists only across a small space, it can be attached via telephone lines to other LANs over a greater distance. A group of LANs connected in such a way is referred to as a Wide Area Network (WAN).

McKinsey and Company 7-S Model

The model considers the following elements, which are all interrelated:

Strategy

Strategy can be described as a means to ensuring an organisation has a market advantage over the competition. This advantage can be manifested in a number of ways but ultimately advantage is achieved through being, in at least one characteristic, unique.

Strategy has been defined by some authors as follows: "Strategy is, or at least ought to be, an organization's way of saying: 'Here is how we will create unique value'."

Systems

The term "systems" refers to the entire menagerie of methods and procedures put in place within an organisation in order to assist the managing of it. The main objective of systems is to sharpen up the focus of the management team and therefore increase the effectiveness of them along with the organisation overall.

Structure

Structure prescribes how people within an organisation are grouped and indicates where control of that organisation is located. The main reason why structure is put in place is because it can help to increase the efficiency of the business by concentrating the staff's minds on the tasks to be undertaken. When building a structure, the need for division in order to aid depth of specialist knowledge must be offset against the need for maintaining a unified firm.

Structure can be manifested in four main forms: network, matrix, functional and divisional.

Skills

This refers to the particular talents that are held within an organisation. These talents can be held not only by individual members of staff but can also be embedded into the ethos of the company. In the latter scenario it is the company as a whole that possesses and represents good practice in the given area.

Style

Style is not a measurement of the output of an organisation – it is an assessment of the manner in which output is produced. What do managers spend their time doing – for example, are they participating in meetings or supervising the staff? Where is the focus of the managers – is it fixed internally or externally? How are decisions taken – in a top-down or bottom-up manner? The answers to all these questions will point to a certain style that, in turn, lays down the cultural norms of that organisation.

Staff

How a company selects, integrates and develops its staff of course differs greatly between different companies. However, these processes coupled with the demographics of the people the organisation chooses to employ and deployment of particular people to particular areas has a profound effect on the overall performance of it.

Shared values

Shared values refers to the beliefs that are central to the company's ethos and mould the approach that those within the organisation apply in the everyday situations they are faced with. Shared values are useful as they help to maintain concentration on the focal point of the organisation and furnish a feeling of there being a common goal that everyone is working towards.

Neuro Linguistic Programming (NLP)

This is a theory of human behaviour and communication that is applied to study a person's own individual experiences, and seeks to discover why certain people will do what they do. NLP can assist in developing a personalised method of therapy, where the brain is thought of as a computer. This "computer" can be programmed to feel or act in a different way than before. By doing so, the individuals can be assisted in accomplishing their own specific objectives.

Orchard Matrix of Market Attractiveness

This matrix should be employed when a company is considering a move into a previously uncharted market. The purpose of the model is to provide a tool with which firms can measure the appeal of the options available.

Paradigm shift

A paradigm shift is fundamentally a shift in the basic rationale upon which a market is based. For example, computer speed may be considered a rationale for purchasing a computer. If this rationale was replaced by design, this would mean that a shift in paradigm had occurred. The classic example of this is in the disk drive market with the move away from density in the days of mainframes, to size in the era of the portable and handheld.

Pareto Principle

The Pareto Principle is defined as a theory that states that a tiny number of causes are responsible for a large percentage of the effect. This ratio is usually 20/80.

PEST analysis

It is very important that an organisation considers its environment before beginning the marketing process. In fact, environmental analysis should be continuous and feed all aspects of planning. The organisation's marketing environment is made up from:

1. The internal environment, e.g. staff (or internal customers), office technology, wages and finance, etc.
2. The micro-environment, e.g. external customers, agents and distributors, suppliers, competitors, etc.
3. The macro-environment, e.g. **P**olitical (and legal) forces, **E**conomic forces, **S**ociocultural forces, and **T**echnological forces. These are known as PEST factors.

Political factors

The political arena has a huge influence upon the regulation of businesses, and the spending power of consumers and other businesses. You must consider issues such as:

1. How stable is the political environment?
2. Will government policy influence laws that regulate or tax your business?
3. What is the government's position on marketing ethics?
4. What is the government's policy on the economy?
5. Does the government have a view on culture and religion?
6. Is the government involved in trading agreements such as EU, NAFTA, ASEAN, or others?

Economic factors

Marketers need to consider the state of a trading economy in the short and long terms. This is especially true when planning for international marketing. You need to look at:

1. Interest rates
2. The level of inflation and employment level per capita
3. Long-term prospects for the economy Gross Domestic Product (GDP) per capita, and so on.

Sociocultural factors

The social and cultural influences on business vary from country to country. It is very important that such factors are considered. Factors include:

1. What is the dominant religion?
2. What are attitudes to foreign products and services?
3. Does language impact upon the diffusion of products onto markets?
4. How much time do consumers have for leisure?
5. What are the roles of men and women within society?
6. How long are the population living? Are the older generations wealthy?
7. Do the population have a strong/weak opinion on green issues?

Technological factors

Technology is vital for competitive advantage, and is a major driver of globalisation. Consider the following points:

1. Does technology allow for products and services to be made more cheaply and to a better standard of quality?
2. Do the technologies offer consumers and businesses more innovative products and services such as Internet banking, new generation mobile telephones, etc.?
3. How is distribution changed by new technologies, e.g. books via the Internet, flight tickets, auctions, etc.?
4. Does technology offer companies a new way to communicate with consumers, e.g. banners, CRM, etc.?

Porter value chain analysis

This model is complex but the basic tenets of it can be grasped fairly easily. The model's main use is in the refining of company strategy in order to compare favourably with that of the competitors. The model seeks to provide competitive advantage through establishing the areas where the organisation makes profit. Within this model the emphasis is shifted from placing a cost on everything in a traditional way, to calculating the potential to make money or, the value. The advantage of this system is that it exposes the areas where companies compare and contrast effectively, thus highlighting areas of competitive advantage.

Product life cycle

The time span over which a product exists from the initial phases of design until close-out.

Random walk

The idea that all factors are open to an unpredictable future where the value of those factors can increase as well as decrease with equal probability.

Real options

The ability to choose to make a decision, at some point in the future. As the future is uncertain and market conditions can change unpredictably, making one decision can be better or worse than making another. Sydney Howell *et al.*, define it in their book *Real Options*, as: "real option analysis helps to decide: (a) how much money we should spend to acquire an economic opportunity, and (b) when (if ever), we should commit ourselves to one of the available decisions".

Return Material Authorisation (RMA)

The process under which faulty goods are returned to the manufacturer.

Spherical vision

Spherical vision provides a 360-degree view of the organisation and its internal and external relationships.

STORM

At the heart of the GMAS is the STORM. This is a meeting chaired by the strategic planning team which provides the human input into the interpretation of both real-time and right-time market intelligence and supplies the initial decisions. STORM (Strategic Tactical Operational Review Management) is the central key of the principal GMAS module groups: Strategy, Operations, Staff, R-TIME Critical Assumptions, Monitoring, and Testing.

Strategic Business Unit (SBU)

Product lines or businesses that have been tied together inside a company because they share markets, competitors or strategies. SBUs bring under one management various product groupings that had previously been administered separately and were very common in the 1990s. And their staff support services like accounting and technical development can be brought in, too.

SWOT analysis

SWOT analysis is a tool for auditing an organisation and its environment. It is the first stage of planning and helps marketers to focus on key issues. Once key issues have been identified, they feed into marketing objectives. It can be used in conjunction with other tools for audit and analysis, such as PEST analysis and Porter's Five-Forces analysis. It is a very popular tool with marketing students because it is quick and easy to learn.

SWOT stands for strengths, weaknesses, opportunities, and threats. Strengths and weaknesses are internal factors – for example, a strength could be your specialist marketing expertise; a weakness could be the lack of a new product. Opportunities and threats are external factors – for example, an opportunity could be a developing market such as the Internet; a threat could be a new competitor in your home market. During the SWOT exercise, list factors in the relevant boxes. It's that simple.

A word of caution: SWOT analysis can be very subjective. Do not rely on it too much. Two people rarely come up with the same final version of SWOT. So use it as a guide and not a prescription.

Transactional research

Research conducted looking at the customer experience and satisfaction with a specific service or purchase event.

Value-added retailer

A company that sells items that have been produced by another company but prior to retailing the goods, adds something of worth to the package. For example, a company may purchase computers for resale but prior to selling them installs some software, thus increasing the value of the computer.

BIBLIOGRAPHY

Barger, H. (1955) *Distribution's Place in the American Economy Since 1869.* Princeton University Press.

Bonoma, T. & Clark, B. (1988) *Marketing Performance Assessment.* Harvard Business School Press.

Bonoma, T. & Crittenden, V. (1988) Towards a model of marketing implementation, *Sloan Management Review,* 29 (2).

Buzzell, R. & Gale, B. (1987) *The PIMS Principles: Linking Strategy to Performance.* New York Free Press.

Citrine, W. (1995) *The ABC of Chairmanship.* NCLC Publishing.

Drucker, P. (1985) How to measure white collar productivity. *Wall Street Journal.*

Farley, F. (1990) A meta analysis of the Application of Diffusion Theory. *Journal of Marketing Research,* 27, 70–77.

Financial Reporting Council (June 2006) *The Combined Code on Corporate Governance.*

Financial Reporting Council (Nov. 2006) *The UK Approach to Corporate Governance.* Grant Thornton.

Gale, B. (1987) The PIMS Principle. *Harvard Business Review.*

Goodman, P. & Pennings, J. (1977) *New Perspectives on Organizational Effectiveness.* Jossey-Bass, San Francisco. Gratus, J. (1990) *Give and Take.* BBC Books.

Gross, I. (1984) *Marketing Productivity Measurement* (cited in Bonoma & Clark, 1988).

Horan, J. (1990) *One Page Business Plan* (Published in-house).

Huff, D. (1993) *How to Lie with Statistics*. W.W. Norton.

Kotler, P. (1997) *Standing Room Only*. Harvard Business Press.

LeBaron, D. (2002) *Investment Quotations*. John Wiley & Sons Inc., New York.

MacDonald, C. (1982) *The Marketing Audit Workbook*. McGraw-Hill, New Jersey, USA.

Mehrotra, S. (1984) How to measure marketing productivity. *Journal of Advertising Research*.

Michaluk, G. (2000) *GMAS Model: Riding the Storm*. Prentice Hall.

Michaluk, G. (2002) *Riding the Storm*. McGraw-Hill International (UK) Limited.

Moore, G.A. (1995) *Inside the Tornado*. New York Harper Business.

Moore, G.A. (2000) *Living on the Fault Line: Managing Shareholder Value in the Age of the Internet*. New York, Harper Business.

Nadler, G. & Hibino, S. (1999) *Creative Solution Finding: The Triumph of Breakthrough Thinking over Conventional Problem Solving Prima Lifestyles*. Prima Lifestyles.

Norton & Kaplan (2001) *The Balanced Scorecard: Translating Strategy into Action* (p. 93), Harvard Business Press.

Peters, T. & Waterman, R. (2004) *In Search of Excellence*. Grand Central Publishing, New York.

Reichheld, F. (1996) *The Loyalty Effect*. Harvard Business School Press.

Risk Management Services (2006) *Corporate Governance Review*.

Sevin, C.H. (1965) *Marketing Productivity Analysis*. McGraw-Hill, New York.

Taylor, H. & Mears, A. (Internal Publication) *The Right Way to Conduct Meetings, Conferences and Discussions*. The Abbey School of Speakers, London.

INDEX

Index compiled by Terry Halliday